The
Greeks
Had a Word
For It

The Greeks*

*and the Russians and the Japanese and the Dutch...

Had a Word For It

Words You Never Knew
You Can't Do Without

Andrew Taylor

BANTAM PRESS

LONDON • TORONTO • SYDNEY • AUCKLAND • JOHANNESBURG

TRANSWORLD PUBLISHERS
61–63 Uxbridge Road, London W5 5SA
www.transworldbooks.co.uk

Transworld is part of the Penguin Random House group of companies
whose addresses can be found at global.penguinrandomhouse.com

First published in Great Britain in 2015 by Bantam Press
an imprint of Transworld Publishers

A CIP catalogue record for this book
is available from the British Library.

ISBN 9780593075715

Typeset in 10.75/15pt Berkeley by Falcon Oast Graphic Art Ltd.
Printed and bound by Clays Ltd, Bungay, Suffolk.

Penguin Random House is committed to a sustainable
future for our business, our readers and our planet. This book
is made from Forest Stewardship Council® certified paper.

1 3 5 7 9 10 8 6 4 2

For Sam, Abi and Rebecca,
and Lucy, Sophie and Tom

Contents

Foreword

WORDS ARE AMONG THE most important things in our lives – somewhere just behind air, water and food. For a start, they're the way we pass on our thoughts from one to another and from generation to generation. Without words, it's hard to see how mankind could ever have evolved from ape-like creatures grunting at the entrance to a cave and wondering where they were going to find their next meal.

But words do more than that. They help us define our emotions, our experiences and the things we see. Put a name to something and you have started out on the road to understanding it.

To look at the figures, you'd think that we already have more than enough words in English – estimates vary between five hundred thousand and just over two million, depending on how you count them. And most educated people use no more than twenty thousand words or so, which means that we ought to have plenty to spare. Yet we've all had those moments when we want to say something and we can't find exactly the *right* one. Words are like happy memories – you can never have enough of them in your head.

And, maybe most important of all in these days of global interaction, when we need to understand each other more than ever before, words say something about us. If people need a word for a particular feeling, or action, or experience, it suggests that they find it important in their lives – the Australian Aboriginals, for instance, have a word that conveys a sense of intense listening, of contemplation, of feeling at one with history and with creation. In Spanish, there's a word for running one's fingers through a lover's hair, and in French one for the sense of excitement and possibility that you may feel when you find yourself in an unfamiliar place.

Words bring us together. They're precious. And if they're sometimes very funny, too – well, how good is that?

MATTERS OF THE HEART

Physingoomai

(Ancient Greek)

◆

Traditionally, sexual excitement as a result of eating garlic; but in a modern sense, the use of inappropriate adornments to enhance sexual attraction

THERE ARE SOME FOREIGN words the English language clearly needs – the case for them is so obvious that it hardly needs to be put. Others require a little more advocacy on their behalf. Take, for example, the Ancient Greek word *physingoomai* (*fiz-in-goo-OH-mie*).

It refers to someone who gets over-confident and sexually excited as a result of eating garlic. Fighting cocks were frequently fed garlic and onions before a bout because the Greeks – and later cockfight aficionados – believed that it would make the birds fiercer. The idea is that if men were to follow the example of the fighting cocks and gorge on garlic before going on a date, there would be no holding them back.

Whether or not garlic makes men horny, it certainly makes them smelly and thus less pleasant to be close to. As a result, even in these days when programmes about cooking are all over the television and when people seem more than happy to talk publicly about their sexual preferences, it seems unlikely that it is a word that is going to be used frequently outside the rather restricted world of cockfighting. Even the Ancient Greeks don't seem to have required it all that often, since the word itself appears only once in the entire canon of Greek literature, referring to some soldiers from the town of Megara in a comedy by Aristophanes.

In the play, however excited the soldiers get, it's apparent that they are going to have serious difficulties persuading any self-respecting Ancient Greek girls to kiss their garlic-reeking lips. The remedy they have sought to increase their sexual potency at the same time greatly reduces their ability to take advantage of it.

And there lies the clue to why *physingoomai* would be such a useful term in English. Young men who douse themselves in the sort of cheap aftershave that strips the lining from your nasal passages at first whiff; middle-aged men wearing blue jeans so tightly belted around where their waist used to be that their bellies sag opulently over the top; women of a certain age wearing clothes that would have been daring on their daughters – they are all, if they only knew it, falling into the same trap as the Megaran soldiers.

The adornments they have chosen to boost their confidence and make them more attractive to potential partners are exactly the things that will put those partners off. Cheap aftershave, tight belts and sagging bellies, and clothes that have been clearly stolen from your daughter's wardrobe can be as effective as a garlic overdose in keeping people at arm's length. Instead of whatever it was they were hoping for, those who rely on them to enhance their sexual appeal are likely to suffer what we might call a *physingoomai* experience. And there are few more *physingoomai* experiences than showing off by using long words to try to impress someone. Just talking about *physingoomai* could lead to the most humiliating *physingoomai* experience of all.

Cafuné

(Brazilian Portuguese)

◆

Closeness between two people — for example, to run one's fingers tenderly through someone's hair

THINK FOR A MOMENT of the gentleness of affection. It needs a tone and a language of its own – not the urgent, demanding words of love and passion, but gentle, undemanding affection, the sort of love that asks for nothing. It is often so diffident and unassuming that it may sometimes seem to take itself – although never its object – for granted. It may be the warm, safe, family feeling between a mother or father and their child, or the love of grandparents for their grandchildren; perhaps it is the closeness between two people that may some day turn into love, or it may be the relaxed fondness that remains when the fire of a passionate affair has burned low. Either way, it demands its own expression.

In Brazil, they have a phrase that works – *fazer cafuné em alguém* means to show affection of exactly that sort. More precisely, *cafuné* (*caf-OO-neh*) often describes the act of running one's fingers through somebody's hair – possibly lulling them to sleep, or possibly simply expressing a drowsy fellow-feeling. Between two lovers, it might contain the gentlest hint of a sexual promise, precisely capturing the tender longing of the early days of a couple's time together.

At other times, though, the word may be translated simply as 'affection'. Many Brazilians say they are seized by a melancholy nostalgia when they are away from their home and thinking of their family, their religion and their memories. They miss their mother's *rabanada*, a sort of French toast topped with sugar, cinnamon and chocolate that is traditionally served at Christmas; their aunt's *bacalhoada,* or salted cod stew; and their grandma's *cafuné*.

It's not a particularly sentimental word in itself. Some authorities suggest that the gesture originated in a mother's gentle search through her children's hair for fleas and lice, and if that thought isn't enough to quell any incipient sentimen-

Gentle, undemanding affection, the sort of love that asks for nothing.

tality, it's sometimes accompanied by the clicking of the fingernails to mimic the cracking of occasional nits. There's still plenty of affection in the gesture – like two chimpanzees gently grooming each other – though the click of lice's eggs being destroyed is not necessarily a sound you would wish to reproduce on a Valentine's Day card, even if you could.

So it doesn't apply only to humans. You might be gently tickling the head of a much-loved dog or cat, or – Brazilians being well known for their love of horses – stroking the soft, silky hair of a horse's ears. It's a pleasant experience for both the giver and the receiver, and it demands nothing from either of them. So it's a word that describes a state of mind and the action that it leads to – not urgent, not demanding, maybe even slightly distracted and carried out with a mind that is floating aimlessly around other pleasant, undemanding topics. There is room for more *cafuné* in our lives.

Cinq-à-Sept

(French)

◆

The post-work period set aside for illicit love

I N STAID, RESPECTABLE BRITAIN, five o'clock in the afternoon signifies little more than the end of a nine-to-five working day, the peak of the rush hour and the time when a man's chin may begin to bristle with shadow. In France, they do things differently, and with more style.

There, five o'clock marks – or used to mark – the start of *le cinq-à-sept (SAÑK-a-SETT)*, those magical two hours that Frenchmen – or maybe Frenchwomen too, come to that – having slipped away from work, would spend whispering sweet Gallic nothings in the ears of their lovers. Or perhaps that was all part of the stereotype dreamed up by the envious English, who like to believe that everything French, whether it is maids, leave, kisses or knickers, must be slightly naughty.

In any case, by the mid-sixties the French writer Françoise Sagan was declaring in her novel *La Chamade* that this time for lovers was all in the past. 'In Paris, no one makes love in the evening any more; everyone is too tired,' sighed one of her characters.[1] It was not that the country had succumbed to a fit of English morality, just that the preferred time for illicit romance had moved forward in the afternoon to between two and four. *Le cinq-à-sept* had become *le deux-à-quatre*. The French were simply rescheduling their afternoon delight. They were not going to give up what the English referred to vulgarly as their 'bit on the side'. After all, the wife and mistress of President Mitterrand stood side by side at his funeral; Valéry Giscard d'Estaing was rumoured to have so many mistresses that he had to leave a sealed letter saying where he might be found in case of emergency on any particular evening.

Going back further in history, the great nineteenth-century French playwright Alexandre Dumas is said to have returned home unexpectedly to find his wife in bed and, a few moments later, his best friend hiding naked in her wardrobe. With true Gallic flair, he ended up sleeping on one side of his slightly surprised wife, while the lover slept on the other.[2]

It's worth noting that in Canada, where the French speakers have clearly lived for too many years alongside their strait-laced Anglophone compatriots, the phrase has lost its quietly salacious air: if a *Québecois* announces that he is going for a *cinq-à-sept,* he generally means no more than that he is planning to call in at the bar for happy hour.

The metropolitan French are made of sterner stuff. From Calais to the warm beaches of the Mediterranean, the true spirit of *le cinq-à-sept* lives on.

Démerdeur

(French)

◆

Someone who has a talent for getting out of a fix

❖

Drachenfutter

(German)

◆

The apologetic gift brought to
soothe a lover's anger

I T'S PROBABLY INEVITABLE THAT a nation with an idea like *le cinq-à-sept* in its vocabulary should need another one – a word like *démerdeur* (*DAY-MERRD-URR*).

It means literally, with the bluntness of the peasant's cottage rather than the subtlety of *les aristos*, someone who is proficient at getting himself out of the *merde* – a bit of a rascal who may often find himself in trouble but who generally works out a way to extricate himself without too much of a fuss. The French dictionary doesn't list a feminine equivalent – if it did, it would presumably be *démerdeuse* – but there's obviously no reason why women, too, shouldn't be up to no good and similarly adept at avoiding the consequences.

Either way, there is a clear note of admiration about the word. Whatever sin you may have committed – and *démerdeur* is often used about the sort of misbehaviour associated with *le cinq-à-sept* – is more than outweighed by the imagination and dash with which you walk away from it. It's much more direct than the rather prissy English reference to someone who 'always comes up smelling of roses'. Deep down, just about every French man or woman would rather like to be a *démerdeur* or a *démerdeuse*.

In Germany, they do things differently. There, instead of the devil-may-care derring-do of the *démerdeur*, they have the careful planning and guilty foresight of the person who purchases *Drachenfutter* (*DRACKH-en-foot-uh*). *Drachenfutter* means 'dragon-fodder', and it refers to the hopeful gift, whether it be flowers, chocolates or a diamond necklace, with which you might attempt to assuage the feelings of a lover you have angered.

There's something sly, underhand and insincere about *Drachenfutter* – a feeling that the person who buys that calculating little present is rather cold-hearted and cowardly. You can bet that they wouldn't call their lover a dragon to their face. You might not

Deep down, just about every French man or woman would rather like to be a *démerdeur* or a *démerdeuse*.

want to get too close to a *démerdeur* either, but at least they sound like fun. You probably wouldn't get many laughs with your *Drachenfutter*.

Do we need either word in English? Well, there are plenty of *démerdeurs* to be found on this side of the Channel. Footballers, musicians, politicians, lawyers – their names are to be found in the papers often enough. As for the less adventurous among us, the number of petrol stations selling sad bunches of wilting roses suggests that there must be quite a big market for *Drachenfutter*.

Koi no yokan

(Japanese)

◆

A gentle, unspoken feeling that you are about to fall in love

I T'S NOT A COINCIDENCE that we talk of 'falling' in love. It's a sudden thing, at least according to the songs – involuntary, inconvenient, irresistible, possibly even disastrous. It's been compared, among other things, to being hit by a freight train. All in all, then, it doesn't sound like a particularly enjoyable experience.

However, it doesn't have to be any of those things. Just ask the Japanese. They have a phrase, *koi no yokan* (*KOY-noh-yoh-CAN*), which tells a very different story. It translates literally as 'premonition of love or desire', and it refers to the sense that you are *about* to fall in love with someone. There is no certainty, no commitment and probably no mutual awareness – certainly nothing is said – but the feeling is there. It's not love, maybe not even desire – but it's the realization that these things could be on the horizon.

The lazy translation into English is sometimes 'love at first sight', but *koi no yokan is* much more delicate and restrained than that. 'Love at first sight' is a shared surrender – glances across a room, strong emotions reflecting each other, a feeling of certainty. It's getting your knife and fork straight into the main course, if you like, without having a starter, perhaps without even looking at the menu. *Koi no yokan*, on the other hand, is an individual sense of what might happen – the other person involved may at this stage know nothing of how you feel. It's the difference between catching the faintest scent on the wind and, as we said before, being knocked down by a train. *Koi no yokan* senses the first tentative tremor of a feeling. It's a surrender, above all, to the magic of potential.

> *Koi no yokan* can be tinged with sadness as well as anticipation.

With *koi no yokan*, you have the feeling of a subtle, almost imperceptible awareness, the sense that it will become an emotion that will eventually grow and develop over time. It's so gentle that you may find, with a shock, that it's been there for some time, somewhere in the back of your mind, without your realizing it.

So subtle is it that it's not even the moment when you stand on the brink of a love affair, wondering whether you have the courage to jump in, like jumping from a rock into a pool – it's more the moment when you wonder whether you might step up to the rock at all.

It might not lead to love immediately, or perhaps at all, and there may be many ups and downs and twists of fate still to come. For that reason, *koi no yokan* can be tinged with sadness as well as anticipation. Once you're on the rock, even if you shiver there nervously for a while, it's hard in the end not to jump in. But at this moment, there's no pressure on you. You could turn and walk away. And be safe. The point about *koi no yokan* is that it makes no promises, stakes no claims. If you do jump, it's your own responsibility – literally a leap of faith.

Having the word doesn't necessarily give us the feeling, but it does help us to recognize it when it happens. And we can never have enough words to describe our emotions.

Hiraeth

(Welsh)

◆

Intense happiness at a love that was,
and sadness that it is gone

❖

Saudade

(Portuguese)

◆

The sense of wistful melancholy experienced
when reflecting on lost love

P EOPLE DO FALL IN love in English, but the language sometimes lacks the means to express the delicate ways in
which the experience can affect us. Love and sadness can
be inextricably intertwined; there may be a dreamy but
intense happiness at the love that was, and regret that it is
gone, all touched with an uneasy sense that maybe it was
never really as perfect as it now seems. If English had a
word for that finely judged balance of emotions when
a lover is wronged or a love is lost, there might be fewer

bad love songs on the radio. The Welsh, however – the earliest occupants of Britain, as they might occasionally remind you – have just such a word.

Hiraeth (*HEER-eth*) is a broader, more all-consuming love. It refers usually to the native Welshman's love of Wales, its valleys, its craggy coastline, its language, its poetry and its history. But this is much more than simply homesickness. When a Welsh baritone like Bryn Terfel sings about the welcome they'll keep in the valleys when you come home again to Wales, he also promises that he'll banish your *hiraeth* with a few kisses. Coming home, he's saying, will assuage the longing that you feel.

It's an empty promise. This is an ache that can never be truly relieved. Because *hiraeth* is also a longing for unattainable past times – for your own childhood or for the historic, much-mythologized past of Wales, the days before the Saxons, or the time of Llywelyn ap Gruffydd in the thirteenth century, or of Owain Glyndŵr in the fifteenth. For many, it could be a longing for the days of Wales as an independent nation.

But what has this to do with second-rate songs on the radio? Well, *hiraeth* can be felt for people, too. *Mae hiraeth arna amdanot ti* would translate as 'I feel *hiraeth* for you.' You might translate it as simply, 'I miss you,' but you would be cutting away all the emotion – handing over a cheap bunch of flowers bought in a supermarket rather than a bouquet, still jewelled with dew, that you picked yourself. The Welsh version means 'I long for you deep in my soul; I long for the way we were, for the things we did together, the places we went, the dreams that we shared – and that we may share no more.' You could write that in a poem. The English version, 'Wish you were here,' you'd put on a postcard.

Welsh isn't the only language to boast such an evocative word. The Portuguese *saudade* (*soh-DAHD*) has been memorably translated as 'the love that's left behind', and it has the same connotations of wistfulness and melancholy nostalgia, whether focused on a place or a person. Back in the seventeenth century, the aristocratic soldier-poet Francisco Manuel de Melo caught its knife-edge sense of mingled pleasure and pain with his definition: 'A pleasure you suffer, an ailment you enjoy' – a phrase that could apply just as well to *hiraeth*.

Any Welshman will tell you that the difference between the Welsh language and the English language boils down to the fact that Wales is a romantic land of bards, poets and seers, while English is spoken by accountants in suits. But an Englishman might point defensively to the poetry of A. E. Housman and his 'Land of Lost Content' – 'The happy highways where I went, and cannot come again.'[3] So an Englishman can feel *hiraeth*, even if he doesn't have a word for it.

Mamihlapinatapei

(Yaghan, Tierra del Fuego)

◆

Describes the delicious uncertainty of the early
days of what may or may not become a love affair

F EW THINGS, PARTICULARLY EMOTIONS, are black and white.
Today, you may rather like someone who yesterday
interested you only slightly. Tomorrow or the day after, you
may enjoy their company even more, and sometime after
that, you may fall in love. And in between each of those
stages are a million shades of emotion, affection and desire
that poets have struggled for centuries to define.

It's not an area that English words are very good at
capturing. The more complex our feelings, the more likely
we are to have to create phrases, even sentences, to reflect
them adequately – which is what poets and writers do for a
living. But how wonderful to have one word that describes
a single, nervous, shared moment at the beginning of that
long and delicate process of falling in love – and how tragic
that the language that provided it is now almost certainly
extinct.

Yaghan, once spoken on the remote archipelago of
Tierra del Fuego, is believed to have been one of very few
languages in the world without external influences or

connections with any other language on earth. It grew and developed on its own. It was spoken only by a few islanders at the very tip of South America, so far from anywhere that the islands knew only very occasional visitors, and over the last century or so it has been vanishing almost without trace – a language, a history and a culture lost as if they had never existed. The last known native speaker is now in her late eighties. Little is understood about the structure, grammar or vocabulary of Yaghan, beyond the existence of a rudimentary dictionary published in the late nineteenth century.

But one word survives: *mamihlapinatapei* (*MAH-michk-la-pin-a-TA-pay*, where the *chk* is pronounced at the back of the throat, like the Scottish *loch*). It refers to an unspoken understanding between two people, both of whom want to start something but who are each reluctant to make the first move. It's very like the Japanese *koi no yokan*, then, except that this is essentially a feeling which two people share from the very start. It's not certain whether it relates specifically to the beginning of an affair, but its relevance to those early moments where each one wonders how committed or willing the other might be is clear. It's a word that oozes uncertainty and potential.

Many translations suggest that *mamihlapinatapei* includes a wordless exchange of glances, but even that seems to be too specific for this ghostly word, which seeks to pin down a moment that vanishes like mist. It's not even certain whether it is a noun or a verb.

And the point about *mamihlapinatapei* is that it may *not* relate to the beginning of an affair, or of anything at all. Both the people involved are uncertain about what will happen next – it's perfectly possible that nothing will and that the moment the word describes will remain one of the wistful might-have-beens that gather around the fringes of our memories.

Generally, we seek to pin words down to a particular meaning, the more specific the better. Vagueness in language is often seen as a lack of accuracy, and you would expect a legal document or a set of building instructions to be clear, concise and unambiguous. But what about when the situation you are seeking to describe is vague and uncertain? *Mamihlapinatapei* captures the delicacy of a subtle and nuanced moment in a way that in English would demand a sentence or a few lines of a poem.

STICKS AND STONES . . .

Attaccabottoni

(Italian)

◆

A bore whose only topic of conversation is him- or herself

SAMUEL TAYLOR COLERIDGE'S POEM *The Rime of the Ancient Mariner* tells the tale of a guest hurrying to a wedding who unwisely catches the eye of a mysterious bearded stranger and as a result sits through 143 verses of his story and misses the ceremony. It's an experience you may have had – usually without the benefit of hearing at first hand one of the great classics of English literature – when you've been buttonholed by charity collectors, religious enthusiasts or political canvassers.

If only you had known the Italian word *attaccabottoni* (*at-ACK-a-bot-OH-ni*). Once you can name a danger, it's easier to face it down, and you could have stared the stranger fearlessly in the eye, dismissively murmured, '*Attaccabottoni*', and walked on by. It means a buttonholer, and it refers to the type of bore who manoeuvres you into a corner and proceeds to tell you the long, tedious and apparently endless story of their life, their failed relationship, their children's success with the violin, or the massive problems they've solved single-handedly at work . . . The one thing it will always be about is them, and how cruelly and unfairly they have been treated.

It might be foolish to waste too much sympathy on Coleridge, however. His friend, the essayist Charles Lamb, used to tell a story about him which amounts to a perfect description of an *attaccabottoni*. Coleridge had a habit of holding on to the coat button of the person he was talking to, to impress him with the urgency of what he was saying. Then, eyes closed and making languid gestures with his other hand, he would launch into his story, without a pause for breath. Lamb claimed to have put up with this assault on his time and patience for several minutes on one occasion before he took drastic action.

A true *attaccabottoni* finds nothing remotely interesting but himself.

'I saw that it was no use to break away so . . . with my penknife I quietly severed the button from my coat and decamped. Five hours later and passing the same garden on my way home, I heard Coleridge's voice and, looking in, there he was with closed eyes, the button in his fingers, and his right hand gently waving, just as when I left him.'[4]

The tale sounds pretty unlikely, but it's the sort of anecdote that *ought* to be true, if only because it reflects the feelings of so many of us when we are in a hurry to be somewhere but can't bring ourselves to be rude enough to walk away. The only difference is that Coleridge was a dear friend of Lamb's, and this story is told with a good-humoured affection that few of us feel for the earnest doorstep preachers who occasionally keep us from our dinner.

It's easy to tell if you have just been the victim of a common or garden bore or of a dedicated and skilled *attaccabottoni*. Conversations should be a matter of give and take; if, as you limp away wearily from your encounter, you have a nagging feeling that you have learned a lot about the other person but said very little about yourself, then you can be sure that you have suffered at the hands of a master. A true *attaccabottoni* finds nothing remotely interesting but himself. Or herself – the noun can be masculine or feminine in Italian.

It might be possible to feel a degree of sympathy for an *attaccabottoni* – anyone who has to clap you in irons to make you stay and listen is unlikely to have a lot of friends. But you should harden your heart – your attacker is exploiting your own decency and good manners and turning them into weapons against you. It would be easy enough to tell them to shut up and walk away, if only you were ruder than you are. If by using the word *attaccabottoni* – which they won't understand anyway – you can make yourself feel better about hurrying past, then you will have saved valuable minutes of your life and done no harm.

Davka

(Hebrew)

•

A gruff, one-word response to someone in authority

THERE IS ALWAYS ROOM in a language for one more word, which, with its surly defiance, its refusal to engage, its sheer unreason, enables teenagers to drive adults to impotent distraction. One like the English word 'Whatever', which says, 'Yes, I've heard you, but I'm not interested, I'm not going to pay any attention, and I'm going to keep doing exactly what it was that you said I shouldn't.'

A word, perhaps, like the Hebrew *davka* (*DAV-ka*). It is a word with a long history, its roots reaching back into the ancient Middle Eastern language of Aramaic. It is used in the Jewish Talmud and in rabbinical commentaries on it to mean 'precisely' or 'in this way and no other'. *Matzah*, for instance, the unleavened bread traditionally eaten during the Passover holiday, is made *davka* from wheat, barley, spelt, rye and oats. No other grains will do.

Today, *davka* retains that meaning, but it has also gathered a sense of deliberation and contrariness, so that it often has a sarcastic overtone. English sometimes pulls the same trick with the word 'precisely' – 'Do you know how many biscuits he'd left me in the tin? Precisely one.' The implication is that you might have hoped for more than that, but one was all you got, and that's pretty much just as you'd expect.

Davka can have much the same 'Just like him' edge to it – 'I asked for a red shirt, so, *davka*, he bought me a blue one' – but it often has a wider implication that the world as a whole is being cruel to you. Fate is not on your side – 'I was in a hurry, so, *davka*, the bus was late.' A child who is said to be 'doing *davka*' is being contrary and difficult, in the way that children can be.

So the word has a variety of meanings, which English might try to pick up in several different ways. But the one that might be most useful – the one that Israelis speaking English say they miss most – is when it is used as a gruff, one-word response to someone in authority. In English, if you ask your surly teenage son where he is going, you might get the answer, 'Out.' Or if you ask your daughter what she has in her bag, 'Stuff.'

So in Hebrew, you might ask, 'Why are you doing that?' and get the answer, '*Davka*' – because I choose, because I want to do it this way rather than any other. Just because. It's about expressing determination, independence and a degree of contempt, all in one word.

And don't we all have a little bit of teenager in us every now and then?

Ilunga

(Tshiluba, Democratic Republic of Congo)

◆

A willingness to let an offence go twice but never a third time

*I*LUNGA (*IL-UNG-AH*) HAD ITS fifteen minutes of fame back in 2004, when the BBC reported that it had been chosen as the world's most untranslatable word in 'a list drawn up in consultation with 1,000 linguists'. Oddly, the article then went on to translate it with some confidence as 'a person who is ready to forgive any abuse for the first time, to tolerate it a second time, but never a third time' – which seems to suggest that it's actually quite straightforward to translate, if a little lengthy.

The idea of a word being the hardest to translate is a bit strange anyway – certainly until you've defined which language you're translating into. A word that's hard to translate into English may have a perfect equivalent in Korean or Welsh.

A gradual, even unwilling diminution of sympathy.

Ilunga comes from the Bantu Tshiluba language, spoken by some six million people in the southern region of the Democratic Republic of Congo. Other commentators weighed in to the BBC immediately with their own suggestions, including several who put forward the American saying 'Three strikes and you're out' as an equivalent.

For anyone who knows nothing about the rules of baseball, that sentence would itself be pretty hard to translate, and that fact seems to highlight one of the most intractable difficulties of translation. It's all very well to replace one word with another – a *carretilla* in Spain, or a *schubkarre* in Germany, would probably look very much like a wheelbarrow in England – but it's the unspoken assumptions and cultural implications that go with a word that can make it almost impossible to replicate in a different language.

'Three strikes and you're out' has a threatening ring to it – an implication that justice is implacable and inevitable. The rules of baseball, after all, are very clear and brook no argument on the subject, which is the reason for carrying the phrase into the administration of the criminal law: there will be no argument and no plea in mitigation. It might even sound rather smug.

That's certainly not the case with the meaning of *ilunga*, which describes a gradual, even unwilling diminution of sympathy. The emphasis is on the mercy that is shown at first, rather than on the condemnation that will eventually follow – precisely the opposite of 'Three strikes and you're out.'

It may be unrealistic to think that we are such a patient and forgiving people that we need a word which suggests that our first instinct in response to any injury would be forgiveness, and that our preference is always to show mercy until the offender has demonstrated once and for all that he is just going to take advantage of our gentleness. But it's a very nice idea.

Schlimazl & Shlemiel

(Yiddish)

◆

Someone prone to accidental mishaps & someone clumsy who creates their own mishaps

WE ALL HAVE MOMENTS when it seems as if the world is ganging up against us – moments when we've spent an hour getting ourselves ready for an important occasion, with a new suit and freshly polished shoes, only for a car to drive past through a puddle and cover us with mud. Moments when we've written a particularly fine letter on our computer and are just about to print it out when there's a power cut. Moments when we sit down on a broken chair that collapses beneath us, or lean against a door that's just been painted.

We all go through those Charlie Chaplin experiences that would seem very funny if only they were happening to someone else but are near-disasters when they happen to us. For most of us they don't *really* happen all that often – it just feels as if they do. But suppose they happened to you all the time – what would you be then, apart from suicidal?

For some people, petty disasters do seem to be a way of life. And if you're one of them, you're a *schlimazl* (*shli-MAZL*). It's an old Yiddish word that means someone who is chronically unlucky, someone to whom bad things happen all the time. These mishaps are probably nobody's fault, and they're not tragedies, not disasters that are going to ruin a person's life, but they are the ridiculous little accidents that can drive you to distraction. Why me, you say.

However, it could be worse. Suppose it was all your *own* fault? Rather than have a random car drive past and soak you, you might have tripped over into the puddle all by yourself, stumbling over the shoelace you hadn't tied properly. Instead of a power cut, you might have lost your beautifully crafted letter because you'd turned off the computer by accident. Maybe the chair was fine, but you were just too heavy for it. And how much more annoying would it have been if you'd painted the door yourself?

In those cases, it would be your own foolishness or clumsiness that was to blame, and instead of being a hapless *schlimazl* you'd be a hopeless *shlemiel* (*shlum-EEL*). At least if you're a *schlimazl*, when people have finished laughing at you, they'll feel a moment of sympathy for your hard luck. If you're a *shlemiel*, a person who is so clumsy and awkward that you only have to pick up something fragile to drop it, then the chances are that the only response you're likely to get will be a sneering 'Serves you right.'

And there are refinements of this miserable fate. Sometimes the *shlemiel* will resent the reputation he has acquired so much that he will try to do ambitious things that even someone who is not naturally clumsy would avoid, just to prove that he's not as clumsy as everyone thinks. He – or she – will carry tottering piles of plates and glasses, or scoff at the idea of putting down a piece of news-paper before they start painting. The *shlemiel* will balance a bowl of soup on his outstretched fingers and move it around in the air, just to prove that he can. And, of course, he can't. It always ends in tears. Not even Yiddish has a word for such a hopeless case. In fact, the bowl of soup can be used as an example to demonstrate the difference between the two: when the *shlemiel* spills his soup, it lands on the *schlimazl*.

The two words are ideal as light-hearted insults – the sort of remarks that elicit a rueful smile and a shrug of the shoulders from their object, rather than a punch on the nose. Surely a language can never have too many words like that.

Mafan

(Mandarin)

◆

**When it's all too much bother but, to your mind,
not being bothered is not your fault . . .**

WE ALL HAVE THEM – those moments of angst,
world-weariness and frustration when something is
just too much trouble. It may be something we've done a
thousand times before without complaining – taking out
the rubbish, washing the car or taking the dog for a walk.
Suddenly, for no particular reason, it's just one thing too
many and we're not going to do it.

'I can't be bothered,' we might say, and it's likely to
make people cross. And, most of the time, and probably
with ill grace, we somehow end up doing whatever it is that
needs doing.

That's the problem with 'I can't be bothered.' It's a blunt
phrase that, just at a time when you really don't feel like
taking responsibility, puts you right in the firing line.
It's not what you want to say: the problem is with the
suddenly unreasonable demand that is being made, not
with your own response to it. What you want is a phrase
that throws the blame where you instinctively know it
belongs – on the person who has made the request, on the

action itself, on the entire world if necessary, but not on you.

The Chinese have an invaluable little word – *mafan* (*MAH-FAHN*). Some people say that if you learn only one word of Chinese, then *mafan* is the one – although that could be a reflection on the frustrations of Chinese bureaucracy rather than a comment on the word itself.

It means something you've been asked to do is too bothersome – just too much trouble. It's frustrating, annoying and completely unreasonable that you have been asked. But the important thing about it is that it focuses the blame where it should be – not on you.

Its applications are almost infinite. A tax form may be too complicated for anyone but a Professor of Incomprehensible Logic to understand, and you would ask, 'Why is this so *mafan*?' Or it could be used against you in a restaurant, when you ask if you could have the noodles but without the meat – 'No, that's too *mafan* for the chef.'

And the beauty of it is that it's not an exclusively dismissive or negative word. You can apologize – probably insincerely, but no one's to know – for causing someone so much *mafan*. Tack -*ni*, meaning 'you', on to it and it is suddenly an extremely polite and courteous way of asking a question, more or less equivalent to 'Excuse me, may I trouble you?' So you might say, '*Mafan-ni*, could you tell me the way to the station?'

But we do politeness well in English already. We have plenty of ingratiating little phrases with which to butter people up when we want them to do us a favour. It's that subtle evasion of responsibility that we need, that deft avoidance of blame. 'Shouldn't you take the dog for a walk?' '*Mafan*.'

It shouldn't work, of course. It would seem to drip with the same sort of dismissive contempt that an idle teenager can pour over the words 'Whatever,' or 'Yeah, right.' But the Chinese seem to manage *mafan* quite successfully. Perhaps we should give it a go in English.

Pochemuchka

(Russian)

◆

Term of endearment for a child who asks a lot of
questions – perhaps too many questions

'YES, BUT WHY?'
As anyone who has children will know, these words
bring a thrill of joy to our hearts the first time we hear
them, because we are new parents, and idealistic, and
optimistic, and we want to encourage a healthy curiosity
in our offspring. And so we offer a carefully crafted and
well-thought-out explanation, not too simple but pitched
at exactly the right level for our child's understanding.

'Yes, but why?'

The next explanation has a slightly puzzled edge to it.
We thought we'd answered that one the first time. So we try
again.

'Yes, but why?'

The third explanation is probably a little shorter and
slightly less carefully crafted. It might even have a barely
perceptible edge of frustration. There is, after all, a newspaper that we want to read, or a programme to watch, or a
car to polish.

'Yes, but why?'

The fourth explanation is even shorter. It may well contain an unfortunate phrase like 'For God's sake!' in it, or possibly something even less acceptable. And so it goes on, six or seven times or more, until, to our eternal shame, we come through clenched teeth to the final and unavoidable, 'Because I say so!'

> The diminutive suffix -*uchka* makes clear that it's meant affectionately.

This child with the healthy curiosity that we were once so keen to encourage is what the Russians would call a *pochemuchka* (*POH-chay-MOO-chka*) – someone who asks too many questions. It comes from the Russian word *pocemu* (*POH-chay-MUH*), which means 'Why?', and was first used in a popular Soviet-era children's book[5] whose hero was a little boy given the nickname Alyosha Pochemuchka because he was never satisfied with the answers he got. The book was published in 1939, when Stalin was at the height of his power, so discouraging children from trying to find out too much was probably a wise move for cautious parents, but it's generally the sort of light-hearted put-down that might be expressed in English with a warning like 'Curiosity killed the cat.'

The diminutive suffix -*uchka* makes clear that it's meant affectionately, but do we really need a word like this? Once we've got over the frustration of a long train of 'Yes, but whys', we don't *really* want to tell our children not to ask too many questions.

But the term doesn't *have* to be applied only to

children. It may not be a clever way to address a Russian policeman who is asking you for details of where you've been and whom you've seen, but assimilated into English it might be a very useful word to use to a local government official who won't go away, or anyone in authority for whom it would be much less aggressive than a bad-tempered 'Mind your own business.' That patronizing *-uchka* at the end, the verbal equivalent of patting the person you are speaking to on the head, might also give a very pleasant feeling of superiority.

Schnorrer

(Yiddish)

◆

Someone very skilled at getting others to pay out of a sense of duty

MAKE THE MISTAKE OF getting out of a taxi without leaving a big enough tip and you may hear the taxi driver mutter under his breath, 'Schnorrer!' (SHNORR-uh). This, you will understand instinctively, is not a compliment.

Originally, the word was used by Jews about Jews, describing a dishonest beggar – a man, for example, who might dress as a gentleman, talk with all the pretensions of a scholar and treat his companion with expansive and condescending civility, but who would still ask for the loan of the price of a phone call. And then ask again. And again for something else.

Such a man would give elaborate and generally entirely imaginary reasons for asking for help – he might have been robbed, his house might have burned down, or he might find himself temporarily embarrassed at a moment when he needs to pay to get his car mended, settle an annoying bill, or offer assistance to a relative who has fallen on hard times. In any case, since both the schnorrer and generally his victim as well are Jewish, there is an overriding moral duty to help him. The more emotional and affecting the story, the better.

A particular kind of *schnorrer*, the *literary schnorrer*, might offer copies of a book he has written – always a literary masterpiece, in which he has selflessly invested years of hard and unrewarded work – in return for whatever gift of money the wealthy recipient thinks appropriate. And if the gift is not large enough, the *schnorrer* is likely to make it very clear that he is unimpressed.

Rather than sitting at the roadside asking for alms, the *schnorrer* engages with his target, giving the impression that he expects support as of right and is actually conferring a favour by offering the opportunity to give him money or goods. The frequent translation 'beggar' fails to reflect the impudence and presumption of the true *schnorrer*, whose shameless audacity is best summed up in another Yiddish word, *chutzpah* (*HOOT-spa*). Other words like 'sponger', 'chiseller' or 'freeloader' miss the all-important element of entitlement, while 'con man' or 'confidence trickster' do not include the sense of duty that the true *schnorrer* seeks to instil in his victim.

The English writer Israel Zangwill, working at the end of the nineteenth century, published a satirical novel named *The King of Schnorrers*, which tells the story of a Sephardic Jew, the grandly named Manasseh Bueno Barzillai Azevedo da Costa, who plays on his claims of scholarship, family background and royal connections to fleece a succession of more or less gullible victims. More ironically, the Zionist leader Theodor Herzl, around the same time, said that the best-kept secret of his campaign was the work of 'an army of *schnorrers* possessing a dream' who hassled and persuaded and cajoled Jews across Europe to support his idea of a Jewish state.

Your taxi driver is probably not remembering these literary antecedents and probably not even thinking of the traditional characteristics of the Jewish *schnorrer.* He is simply using the best word available to describe a tightwad, a miser, a Scrooge and a skinflint, all rolled together and invested with all the contempt, mockery and derision that the Yiddish language can muster.

Or nearly all. If you don't leave any tip, you may hear the word *schnorrerdicke* (*SHNORR-uh-DICK-uh*). That means the same, but much, much more so. Better by far to give him his tip in the first place – and make it a big one.

Handschuhschneeballwerfer & Sitzpinkler

(German)

◆

A man who is a bit of a wimp

FEW NATIONAL STEREOTYPES CAN be as undeserved as the reputation that the Germans have picked up for having no sense of humour. How can that possibly be true of a people who speak a language with words that are seventy-nine letters long? Their habit of creating a new compound word by the simple expedient of sticking together two, three, four or more old ones would seem logically to mean that German can translate any number of words in any language with just one of its own.

Practical stuff. But how could you use a word like *Donaudampfschiffahrtselektrizitätenhauptbetriebswerkbau-unterbeamtengesellschaft* without sniggering? It means 'The association for junior officials of the head office management of the Danube steamboat electrical services', and if any journalist were ever foolish enough to use it, it would run into three lines of a single column in a broadsheet newspaper – not that it crops up much in conversation. I suspect that, like its rather less impressive English equivalents *antidisestablishmentarianism* (opposition to a policy of taking away the Church of England's special role in the state) or *floccinaucinihilipilification* (the act of valuing something as practically worthless), *Donaudampfschiffahrt* etc. is one of those words cobbled together simply to give schoolchildren something to laugh and marvel at.

So the German language's capacity for making new compounds from old words results in more than just astonishing length. It also gives the language an enviable sense of fun. Take *handschuhschneeballwerfer* (*hant-shoo-SHNAY-ball-vairf-uh*) and *sitzpinkler* (*SIT-spink-luh*), for instance. Each of them arrives at pretty much the same meaning, although they take a different route to get there. And you probably wouldn't want either of them to be applied to you.

A *handschuh* is, literally, a 'hand-shoe' – a glove. (If you couldn't work that out for yourself, you haven't got into the spirit of compound words.) *Schnee* is snow, so *schneeball* is pretty obvious; and the verb *werfen* is what you do to one. So a *handschuhschneeballwerfer* is a person who wears gloves to throw snowballs. That is not interpreted, as you might think, as someone who has at least an ounce of common sense but as someone who is scared to get his hands cold – hence, a bit of a wuss, a wimp or a softy.

These days you wouldn't translate that word into English as 'a big girl'. For *sitzpinkler*, however, that might just be an ideal translation. A *sitz* is a seat, and *pinkeln* is what you might do privately while you were sitting down, if you happen to be a woman. (I'm making an effort to be delicate here.) So a *sitzpinkler* is a man who sits down to pee, hence a man who behaves like a woman, and hence – well, someone who's not very macho in a patriarchal society where real men used to show off their duelling scars.

In an English conversation, each of these two words has the advantage of being mildly insulting in a way that won't be understood and therefore won't get you into trouble. But, if you are sufficiently sexist to want to use *sitzpinkler* as a term of abuse, you should be warned that times are changing. In these metrosexual days, it might actually be taken as a compliment. Signs have appeared in some German toilets warning that *stehpinkeln* (the opposite of *sitzpinkeln*) is messy and antisocial. Gadgets exist that play a recorded message to that effect every time a defiant man raises the seat. These warnings come in a variety of voices, including those of the former chancellors Helmut Kohl and Gerhard Schröder.

Imagine some British manufacturer bringing out a similar gadget using the voices of Margaret Thatcher, Tony Blair or David Cameron. But maybe that would be taking the cliché of the nanny state just a bit too far.

Soutpiel

(Afrikaans)

◆

Scorn expressed at someone else's inability to commit fully to something you believe in passionately

SOMETIMES, JUST SOMETIMES, IT'S necessary to be vulgar to get your point across with sufficient force. Take the occasions, for instance, when you are fully committed to an idea or a project, and you have poured yourself heart and soul into ensuring its success. There will be no second thoughts for you – you have burned your bridges, and you're not looking back.

Perhaps it's a minor issue, like playing for a football team or joining a political party, or perhaps it's something life-changing, not just for you but for generations to come – something like building a nation, for instance.

You'll hope that your commitment will inspire others to follow you – if it doesn't, you may be doomed to failure – but you expect those who follow to feel the same level of enthusiasm and single-mindedness when they join as you had right at the beginning. Instead, as the venture begins to show the first signs that it is going to work, you find people flocking to reap the fruits of your hard work while carefully preserving their way out in case things go wrong.

Instead of diving in alongside you, they are constantly looking back nervously over their shoulders, ready to pull out and run for cover the first time things take a turn for the worse.

What's the word you would choose to describe such people? 'Freeloaders' might do, except that it doesn't carry the sense of cowardly retrospection that you are looking for. 'Fainthearts' the same – and neither one begins to touch the contempt and ridicule that you want to express.

That is the problem, early in the twentieth century, which faced the Afrikaaner farmers of South Africa – a people who, with some justification, did not enjoy a good press during much of that century. They felt that the English settlers who had flooded out there after the Boer War were never wholeheartedly committed to the future of South Africa, that they maintained close links to Europe, with property and investments 'back home' as an insurance policy in case they needed to cut and run.

'*Soutpiel*,' (*SOHT-peel*) some leathery-faced old Boer must have spat into the dust as he chewed his biltong. The word means literally, in Afrikaans, 'salt-dick', and at that moment he gave to the world the memorable image of someone standing with one foot in South Africa and the other in England, his legs stretched so that his penis dangled in the sea. The same thought might apply today to those in England who want to stay in the European Union but defend Britain's right to do things differently, or perhaps the many celebrities who seem to live on both sides of the Atlantic at once.

Today, *soutpiel* has been softened into the almost affectionate '*soutie*' (*SOHT-y*), and in town if not in the rural Afrikaaner heartland, English-speaking South Africans may even sometimes use it to describe themselves.

Other former colonial nations have coined their own less-than-respectful names for the citizens of the mother country. The Americans have *limey*, a contemptuous reference to the lime juice that would be added to the Royal Navy's rum ration during the nineteenth century – a sneer that rather backfired, as the vitamin C in the lime juice did at least keep the sailors free from scurvy and the oozing wounds, loose teeth, jaundice, fever and death to which it led.

In Australia, no one really knows where the term *Pom* comes from, though there have been several unconvincing explanations such as *Pomegranate*, describing the colour that the fair-skinned English went in the sun, or P.O.H.M.S., short for Prisoner of Her Majesty's Service. The Scots have *Sassenach*, which means Saxon, not necessarily affectionately, and shows what long memories the Celts have.

But nothing matches the scorn and derision of that vivid Afrikaaner image of the Englishman stretching desperately to keep a foot in both countries, with his pride and joy dangling disconsolately in the chilly waters of the South Atlantic.

Elusive Emotions

Aware

(Japanese)

◆

A sense of the fragility of life

Y OU MIGHT, ON A walk in late summer, see a leaf gently float down to the ground from a high branch. Perhaps you may come downstairs one morning to see that the vase of flowers that last night looked so fresh and full of life has begun to lose its petals. Or you might watch the reds and golds of a beautiful sunset gradually fade away as the sun sinks in the sky.

Any of those experiences might bring you a feeling that the Japanese would call *aware* (*ah-WAH-reh*) – a deep sense of beauty, coloured by the realization that what you are looking at is fragile and fleeting. It is this sense of the impermanence of beauty that lies at the heart of *aware*.

For the Japanese, it is often expressed in the aesthetic concept of *mono no aware*, which translates roughly as 'the pathos of things'. Nearly seven hundred years ago in *Tsurezuregusa*, or *Essays in Idleness*, the Japanese poet and hermit Yoshida Kenkō observed that if people lived for ever, then material things would lose their power to move us. 'The most precious thing in life is its uncertainty,' he said.[6]

For the Japanese, one very common expression of *aware* is in the contemplation of the cherry blossom, which usually lasts only a few days before it begins to fall. In the parks and gardens of Tokyo, silent groups will gather in early April just to look at the array of blossom on the trees as the flowers slowly wilt and die. Coincidentally – and showing that emotions are universal, even though English may lack the precise words to express them – back in late nineteenth-century England, the shy, buttoned-up poet A. E. Housman also chose the cherry blossom to express his own sense of the fragility of beauty and of human life.

In the poem 'Loveliest of Trees', at the age of twenty, with only fifty years remaining of his allotted span, he says:

> And since to look at things in bloom
> Fifty springs are little room,
> About the woodland I will go
> To see the cherry hung with snow.[7]

The spring blossom has turned in his mind to the snow of winter – a chilly symbol of mortality. The mixture of appreciation, thoughtfulness and regret comes close to the heart of the meaning of *aware*.

The cycle of the seasons, with growth, maturity and death exhibited in falling petals and dying leaves, is the traditional way to demonstrate *aware*, but it applies throughout life. A glimpse of a faded photograph on an old woman's mantelpiece showing her as a young bride; the dry, curled pages of a precious childhood book; a crisp, shrivelled leaf about to crumble away into nothingness – all these could inspire the same wistful sense of inescapable mortality.

There is sadness, but it is a calm, resigned sadness, and it is coupled with a humble acceptance of the beauty of existence. Perhaps the whole concept might seem maudlin at first glance, except that the concentration is not on death and the end of everything but on the fact of its existence. It is a bittersweet emotion but essentially a positive and life-affirming one.

Cocok

(Javanese)

•

A perfect fit

SPEAKERS OF ENGLISH, IT seems, would like to be seen as a tolerant, non-judgemental, open-minded lot. We have the phrases and proverbs to prove it: 'One man's meat is another man's poison', 'Each to his own', 'You pays your money and you takes your choice'. We are not going to be dogmatic about what is best or worst, we are saying: people have their own preferences, and we respect them.

But if the non-judgemental self-image were true – if we really were so unwilling to lay down the law and tell other people what they should think – surely we would have a single word to express the idea, rather than having to rely on a few hackneyed clichés? A word we could use, for example, if someone asked us if we knew a good restaurant, or if a book was worth reading, or whether a particular model of car was any good.

As it is, we can say the restaurant, the book or the car are good, or bad, or somewhere in between, and we may think we're being helpful. But the truth is that you may hate the sort of food that someone else enjoyed in the restaurant, you may be bored by the book that they found fascinating, and you may find the car that they drive and love a bit uncomfortable and old-fashioned. We each have our preferences.

What we need is a word like the Javanese *cocok* (*cho-CHOCH*, with the final *ch* pronounced as in the Scottish *loch*).

An inadequate translation into English might be 'suitable', although *cocok* can be either an adjective or a verb: a thing can be *cocok* or it can *cocok*. I could say that the restaurant, or the book, or the car would be *cocok* for you – that you would like them. But that is only scratching the surface of this fascinating and beautiful word. One leading anthropologist has suggested that *cocok* means to fit like a key in a lock, or to be exactly right, like the medicine that cures a disease. Javanese villagers might say that their greatest ambition for their children is that they should find a job which is *cocok*. If two people agree in such a way that the view of each one not only supports the other but brings to it subtleties and nuances that the other person had not thought of, then their opinions will be *cocok*.

In its purest sense, the word means that two things fit together so perfectly that each one gains meaning and value from the other: together, they are greater than the sum of their parts. It has its philosophical roots in Kejawen, a Javanese synthesis of Islam, Hinduism, Buddhism and animism, which sees the whole of creation as an intricate fitting together of its disparate parts – everything visible and invisible, past, present and future. That is the aim both of the individual soul and of creation itself; everything that is *cocok* is part of a greater, eternal metaphysical harmony.

If that sounds a rather grandiose way to express a preference for one restaurant over another, a liking for a particular book, or the choice of one car above all others, then that's probably because you haven't bought into the concept. The Javanese themselves might use *cocok* to describe their food, their clothing, or even their government. And, after all, however good a restaurant meal may be, left alone it will simply congeal and go mouldy; eaten, it will become part of you, while you will have a satisfied, fulfilled feeling of well-being and grow strong and healthy.

But perhaps if English speakers can't accept the world view from which the word comes, then English doesn't really need the word. Certainly, anyone who asks in English if a car is any good will look a bit strangely at you if you tell them it's *cocok*; maybe the sense of oneness with the harmony of the eternal universe is a cultural step too far for us to take in our daily lives.

Except . . .

If you are lucky enough to have found the partner who is the one person in the world with whom you can envisage spending your life, one who understands you and feels like part of you, then you might one night murmur in his or her ear that they are truly *cocok* and explain what the word means. And then just wait for the result. It beats flowers or chocolates.

Duende

(Spanish)

◆

Visceral or spiritual feeling evoked by the arts

WILLIAM WORDSWORTH OBSERVED THAT poetry had its roots in 'emotion recollected in tranquillity'[8] – that a poet might experience the heights and depths of emotion, but he needed time and calm to transform them into poetry. His words have become inseparable from the English Romantic movement. But they remain only a pale and partial shadow of the Spanish concept of *duende* (*duEND-eh*), which is the soul or spirit at the heart of music, poetry or any artistic performance.

In Spanish and Portuguese mythology, the word referred to a sprite or fairy that might play tricks on travellers astray in the forest, or sometimes to a more sinister red-robed skeletal figure who carried a scythe and presaged death. Those whom he visited could sometimes be inspired, in their fear and mental turmoil, to heights of creative brilliance. That quality of inspiration is at the heart of the word's more modern meaning.

According to the twentieth-century Spanish poet Federico García Lorca, other inspirations for creativity – the muses or the angels – come from outside the artist, but *duende* comes from deep within. It needs, Lorca said, 'the trembling of the moment, and then a long silence' – a little like Wordsworth's thought, then. *Duende*, though, goes much further. For artists or performers, it may produce a moment of shattering brilliance, a complete absorption in their art, like the abandoned ecstasy of a Spanish dancer; and without it, the most technically perfect production will be lifeless, without soul. In his 1933 lecture, 'Play and Theory of the Duende',[9] Lorca tells the story of an accomplished singer being told: 'You have a voice, you understand style, but you'll never ever succeed because you have no *duende*.'

The ghostly scythe still lurks in the background. For Lorca, *duende* would only truly manifest itself when there was also an instinctive awareness of the possibility and inevitability of death. The artist could only live fully in the moment when he knew deep in his soul that it could be the *last* moment. Lorca linked *duende* with the passion of the Spanish bullring, but he believed that all Spanish art, particularly the performing arts of music and dancing, was inextricably linked with the contemplation, the fear and the glorification of death. Other artists, though, see *duende* as a quieter, more peaceable manifestation of unrepeatable and often inexplicable artistic brilliance. The Australian musician Nick Cave, for instance, says that it involves 'an eerie and inexplicable sadness', and refers to the music of Bob Dylan, Leonard Cohen, Van Morrison and Neil Young.

'All love songs must contain *duende*, for the love song is

never truly happy,' he said at a lecture in Vienna in 1999. 'Within the fabric of the love song, within its melody, its lyric, one must sense an acknowledgement of its capacity for suffering.'[10]

So musicians, singers, dancers and other creative artists may channel *duende* through their work. And for those who experience a work of art – the ones who watch the dancer or hear the music – *duende* will manifest itself as a sudden, potentially life-changing moment of insight, an instant in which time seems to have stopped. It is beyond analysis, beyond explanation, beyond criticism – art experienced in the deepest recesses of the soul.

For many people, Wordsworth's calm prescription still remains the best way to understand the spirit of poetry, the indescribable something that makes it different from prose. The concept of *duende*, however, considers a similar problem in the context of all artistic expression and approaches it from an infinitely more personal, intense and intimate point of view. However it's described, if you've never experienced *duende*, you may never take its meaning fully on board. But if you have, then you will understand the word not just with your brain but in the very pit of your stomach.

Hygge

(Danish)

◆

Emotional warmth created by being with good friends and well-loved family

YEARS AGO THERE WAS a television advertisement for drinking chocolate. It started outside on a chilly winter's night. A lone figure, wrapped up against the cold, was walking briskly down the street, his feet beating a regular rhythm on the paving stones. He was on his way home and, as he got closer, and the night got colder, so the sound of his feet began to quicken, until eventually he was running as fast as he could.

He stopped outside a front door that loomed in front of him, cold and unpromising; he turned the handle, pushed it open and walked inside. And everything changed. Sitting around were his family, with happy, welcoming faces, all luxuriating in the glow of a warming log fire. And there, waiting for him, was a steaming mug of hot chocolate. He wrapped both hands around it with a broad and satisfied smile, and the background music swelled.

It was an advertisement for hot chocolate, which you might think is just a sickly sweet drink that rots your teeth and makes you fat. But it could just as well have been an advertisement for *hygge*.

Hygge (*HEU-guh*) is a Danish word that helps the Danes get through their long, dark winters. It's sometimes translated, inadequately, as cosiness or well-being, but it is specifically about the reassuring emotional warmth, comfort and security that come from being with good friends or well-loved family. The glow of a roaring log burner is often a part of it, but dinner around a restaurant table, with the conversation and laughter swinging easily back and forth, could be *hygge*. So could flickering candlelight, with a glass of wine and a favourite companion, or a favourite seat in a bar or cafe. When the weather doesn't make you warm, *hygge* does, wrapping your love and your friendships around you like a fur coat.

But it's an *emotional* warmth that doesn't necessarily have anything to do with the temperature. Making a snowman with your children – however old they are – is *hygge*. And it doesn't even have to be winter – a Danish summer street festival could be a very *hygge* place to be, with the right company, or a picnic in the open air, or a late-night barbecue. It's all about comradeship and an awareness of the deep and sustaining happiness and sense of security that it brings.

The concept is central to the Danes' image of themselves: to be called a *hyggelig fyr*, or a fellow who is fun to be with, or who inspires a feeling of *hygge*, is about as high a compliment as you can hope for. And to be the opposite – *uhyggeligt* – is to be creepy and scary in a Gothic horror movie kind of way, not just a bit grumpy and unsociable.

The idea of *hygge* gets you through the winter, they say, but it's more than that – it gets you through life.

The traditional English stereotype is all about firm handshakes and a stiff upper lip rather than anything so emotional as *hygge*. But an Englishman might protest that it's easy to misinterpret what seems to be a brusque and buttoned-up handshake. Ruffling your child's hair as he's about to set off for his first day at school, gripping the hand of your son as he boards a plane for a long journey, or squeezing your daughter's arm before you walk down the aisle with her – these could all be very *hygge* moments indeed. We certainly experience it. And now we have a word for it.

Litost

(Czech)

•

Torment caused by an acute awareness
of your own misery and the wider suffering
of humanity in general

THE CZECH REPUBLIC SITS at the vulnerable, much-fought-
over centre of Europe. Through the last century, the
history of the region was largely one of invasion, occupation, tyranny and bloodshed. Under the Nazis in 1939, vast
swathes of Czech territory were incorporated into Hitler's
'Greater Germany' – part of the price Britain and its allies
were prepared to pay for Neville Chamberlain's tragic boast
of 'peace for our time'. The occupation that followed was
bloody and brutal, and so was the liberation. They were
followed at the end of the Second World War by a second
dismemberment, this time by the Soviet Union, and then
forty years of Communist repression, with the brief flow-
ering of the Prague Spring ruthlessly crushed by tanks in
1968.

It's little wonder, with a history like that, that the
Czechs should have come up with a word like *litost*
(*LEE-tossed*).

It is, according to the Czech writer Milan Kundera, 'a

state of torment caused by the sudden sight of one's own misery'. In his novel *The Book of Laughter and Forgetting*,[11] he notes that the long first syllable sounds 'like the wail of an abandoned dog'. Love may be a cure for *litost*, but when the first passionate flush of idealized desire is past, love can also be a source of it. The emotion is, he says mischievously, a torment that is particularly felt by the young, since anyone with any experience of life will know how commonplace and tedious his own self-regarding misery is.

But that's only part of the story. As a novelist, Kundera focuses on the individual – on the student in his novel wallowing in his own unhappiness, for instance. *Litost*, however, can also be a more wide-ranging feeling, a concentration on *our* misery rather than *my* misery. It could be a sudden emotional awareness of the unfitness of things – a realization of the indiscriminate way that death was meted out in the Yugoslav civil wars, of the tsunami-like disaster of the Holocaust crashing down on Europe, or of the succession of miseries that have afflicted the region where the Czechs live. It doesn't have to be as inward-looking as Kundera suggests. But he's correct to point out that it's generally a negative or unproductive emotion that is often followed by the desire for revenge. The rape of Czechoslovakia by the Nazis was followed by the murder of innocent German-speaking civilians at the end of the war.

According to Kundera, *litost* may be dissipated in extreme circumstances by suicide, by violence against the person who has inspired it, or even by provoking them to kill you. For most of us, then, it's definitely not an emotion to be encouraged, since violence, injury and self-destruction are not generally viewed as desirable outcomes.

There is nothing to joke about in the misery of depression, which can strike suddenly, unpredictably and brutally. But *litost* seems somehow self-regarding and posturing, almost like the existential angst of a teenager. Even when *litost* is more wide-ranging, focusing on shared misery, it is still all about the effect of that misery on *me*. Thinking of those who die in conflicts, or the victims of the Holocaust, and agonizing over how unhappy they make *you* feel, seems to lose sight of the point.

There is no English equivalent even though the word describes a state of mind that is more common than we would like to believe. Perhaps we need the word in the language, if only to do our best to avoid the emotion it describes.

Fernweh

(German)

◆

The longing, or need, to be far away – anywhere else

IT WAS A LONG way from home, but there was no doubting his accent. The young man behind the bar in Auckland looked every inch a Kiwi, with his tattooed arms and his All Blacks T-shirt, but his voice said 'West Midlands'. So we exchanged a couple of words as he drew my pint.

'Gap year?' I asked, and he paused for a moment. There was a long, slow grin, and he raised one eyebrow quizzically.

'Gap life, with a bit of luck,' he replied.

The old idea of a gap year as a character-forming break between school and university or between university and the world of work has changed. Now there are sixty-somethings setting off around the world, selling their homes or blowing their pension funds to pay for the journey. And among the youngsters who still make up the vast majority, one year often isn't enough. More and more of them, unenthused by the idea of returning home to fight for insecure jobs in an economy that doesn't seem to want them, are thinking rather of two years, or even more. 'Gap life, with a bit of luck.'

At a time like this we need a word like *Fernweh* (*FAIRN-vee*).

It's a German word that goes back to the twelfth or thirteenth century, and it translates literally as 'far-sickness' – the opposite of *Heimweh*, or 'home-sickness'. It's a desire to travel – not to anywhere in particular, but just to get away, to leave your familiar surroundings and hit the open road. It might last a few months or a few years, or it might consume the rest of your life, but you know that the only way to find yourself is to find new places, new horizons, new experiences. It could describe the feelings of those young and old gap-lifers alike.

Except that there is a darker side to *Fernweh*. The vast majority of travellers set off with a song in their hearts, a joyful wish to get to wherever it is they are going and then perhaps move on again. They are motivated primarily by an optimistic wish to see what the world has to offer. For them, the more familiar wanderlust (another word originally from Germany) might be adequate – as it is for many English translators searching for a suitable rendition of *Fernweh*.

> It might last a few months or it might consume the rest of your life.

The word *Fernweh* was infused with the spirit of the German Romanticism of the early nineteenth century – and, like many of the Romantics themselves, it had a bleak, obsessive edge to it. Without travel, a person who experienced *Fernweh* would feel an overwhelming lassitude, a sadness, a sense of depression that could all too easily develop into a suicidal longing for the last long journey of all. The difference between wanderlust and *Fernweh* is the difference between enjoying a few convivial drinks with your friends and drinking alone, long into the night, because you have to.

Dadirri

(Ngangikurungkurr, Australia)

◆

Contemplation of one's place in the world, involving wonder and humility

THE MANY LANGUAGES OF the Australian Aboriginals are particularly rich in their evocation of the sounds, smells, sights and textures of the natural world, and it's easy to see why. Throughout their 40,000-year history, the Aboriginal peoples have lived in close proximity to the land, and their very survival has depended on their ability to distinguish between one tree and another, to read the likely weather from particular cloud formations, or to recognize specific sounds in the Australian bush.

Many of the Aboriginal languages have no single word for 'tree', but only words for each particular kind of tree; several have words for the smell of rain (*nyimpe* in Arrernte, spoken around Alice Springs, or *panti wiru* in Pitjantjatjara, spoken in Central Australia). They contain a vast repository of practical knowledge about the pharmaceutical and nutritional properties of Australian plants and animals.

But a single word that draws together much of this affinity with the natural world is *dadirri*, from the Ngangikurungkurr language spoken in Australia's Northern

Territory. It's generally translated into English as 'contemplation', but it has a much richer and more spiritual meaning than that. Another translation is 'deep listening', which catches more of the sense of quiet, stillness and attention that the word suggests.

However, it goes far beyond simply listening to the natural world. *Dadirri* might describe the rapt attention paid to the ancient sacred stories about the tribe that have been told or sung for hundreds or thousands of years around a succession of campfires. It might be inspired by the ritual music and dancing of a *corroboree*, at tribal smoking ceremonies, or by the haunting music of the didgeridoo. In that sense – an awareness of the history and culture of the tribe – it can be felt both as the listener and the performer.

Dadirri implies a sense of wonder and humility, an almost mystical awareness of one's individual place in the great mystery of Creation. It focuses attention on both the vastness of the external worlds of time and space, and on the inner thoughts and emotions of the individual as a part of that greater whole.

It is not hard to see why this mystic combination of humility and self-awareness was taken up by Christian churches in the centuries since European explorers arrived in Australia, nor how the identification of the individual with the natural world is relevant to more recent concerns about sustainability and environmental awareness.

There is a growing belief in many English-speaking societies in the benefits of mindfulness, an awareness of the present moment, of your own thoughts and feelings, and of the world around you. Doctors, counsellors, coaches and the NHS recommend it as a way of combatting stress and improving mental well-being.

How much better to be aware of oneself not just in the present moment but in the context of hundreds or thousands of years of history. Several Aboriginal writers and thinkers have suggested that *dadirri* could be the gift of their peoples to modern Australia – an idea and a word whose time has come.[12]

Dépaysé

(French)

◆

Feeling lost, like a fish out of water

S IR JOHN SEELEY WAS a Victorian historian who famously observed that the British, in establishing their empire, seemed 'to have conquered half the world in a fit of absence of mind'. If that's true, then the English-speaking world is composed largely of the descendants of stout-hearted adventurers who sailed round the globe seizing territory without even noticing it. Not, then, people who are hap-piest in their own back garden and feel uneasy anywhere that you need a passport to get to.

And yet, if you search for a word in English to describe the feeling of not knowing quite where you are, not feeling at home, not recognizing your surroundings, you would probably come up with 'disoriented'. 'Bewildered' or 'con-fused' might do instead, or maybe 'befuddled'. All of which suggest an uncomfortable, nervous feeling.

You might think the language that contains these words is one spoken by people who would rather be safe at home, thank you very much, sitting by the fire in that comfy old cardigan with the holes in the elbows, watching *Strictly Come Dancing* while clutching a nice warm cup of hot chocolate – certainly not by the bold and buccaneering descendants of Francis Drake, Captain Cook, or the heroes of the East India Company.

The French have a similar expression, *dépaysé* (*deh-pay-SAY*), which also means lost, or like a fish out of water. *Pays* means country, so the word literally means 'taken out of your country'. But here is the unexpected and, for an English speaker, slightly shaming part: *dépaysé* also has the meaning of feeling disoriented but loving

The excitement of renewal, the relishing of fresh experiences, the idea of a new beginning?

every minute of it. If you are *dépaysé* by a holiday, for instance, it has brought you a change of scenery, reinvigorated you and given you a new lease of life. While the poor old English speaker is still blinking around anxiously for something familiar, like a child looking for his teddy bear, the Frenchman is breathing in the air of freedom, gazing out impatiently at fresh new pastures and relishing the mystery of what might lie over the horizon.

And it goes further than that. The verb *se dépayser* (*suh DEH-pay-say*) literally means 'to exile yourself, to remove yourself from your own country', but it also has the sense of stepping outside yourself, looking at your surroundings with fresh eyes. It's a positive view of unfamiliarity, an acceptance of the fact that living exclusively with what you're used to can have the effect of dulling your senses and quenching your ambitions. There's a similar verb in

French, *se débrouiller* (*suh day-BROO-i-yay*), which has a literal meaning of de-fogging yourself, shaking off the mental baggage that you carry with you and making a new start.

Should we embrace a word to describe a feeling that is shared with the whole of humanity – the excitement of renewal, the relishing of fresh experiences, the idea of a new beginning? Or are we the sort of people who take Marmite and marmalade on holiday with us and want English pubs and fish and chips on the Costa Brava – people who have no time for these fancy foreign ideas?

THE GREAT OUTDOORS

Komorebi

(Japanese)

◆

The magical atmosphere created by sunlight filtering through leaves

I T'S A SPECTACLE THAT'S hard to forget.

The Canal du Midi, cutting through 150 miles of southern France and linking the Mediterranean and the Atlantic Ocean, is an engineering wonder of the seventeenth century. Its creator, Pierre-Paul Riquet, kept around twelve thousand workers on the job with picks and shovels for fifteen years. But it's not the history, or the technological marvels, or even the human triumphs that remain with the traveller – just the staggering, overwhelming beauty of the place.

Sailing through it, the water ahead of the boat is glassy-still, so the reflection of the weathered old stone bridge forms a complete circle, in which it is hard to see where the stone ends and the water begins. The boat noses softly through this magic circle to the other side as if it were a scene from *Alice Through the Looking Glass*. And the silent lines of plane trees, planted for the practical purpose of holding the soil of the banks together, filter the harsh southern sun into a stippled, shivering carpet of light and shadow.

It is one of the most beautiful sights many visitors have ever seen. And there is a Japanese word that describes it exactly.

Komorebi (*KOH-MOH-REHB-i*) is made up of a group of characters which individually signify trees, escape and sunlight, and it's usually translated – or rather described – as sunlight filtering through the leaves. For a simple translation we might try dappled shade, but once you've seen this particular light, you'll realize how inadequate that is.

For a start, it looks at that magical, shimmering atmosphere from a slightly pedestrian angle – at the shade rather than at the light. And, even worse, it concentrates on the pattern on the ground rather than on the quality of the light itself. The Japanese, on the other hand, see the shafts of sunlight shifting and dancing as the leaves move – light escaping from the trees, as the word puts it. *Komorebi* is neither light nor shade, neither sky nor earth, neither movement nor stillness, but the delicate interplay between all of them.

That awareness of light and its subtle creation of atmosphere is a quintessential aspect of the appreciation of nature among the Japanese. A Japanese garden will be a flickering patchwork of light and shade, not just a collection of neatly labelled plants. *Komorebi* provides a gentle, understated hint of the characteristic way in which the Japanese see the beauty of the world about them.

But it's not only the light, the shifting colours and the

delicacy of the scene that *komorebi* celebrates, it's also a beauty of almost unimaginable fragility. The smallest cloud across the sun, a wind any stronger than a light breeze that moves the branches about too violently, and it vanishes as if it had never been there.

And, in that sense, the word applies exactly to the beauty of the Canal du Midi, too. For all Riquet's engineering genius, the canal has proved to be fragile. Along great stretches of the banks, the plane trees that helped to produce that shimmering light are gone, cut down to try to protect the rest from the ravages of an infectious, incurable fungus. Rough-cut stumps line the water's edge like rotten teeth, and the harsh sun beats down without any trembling leaves to lessen its glare. All that is left is the memory of *komorebi*.

Dreich

(Scots)

◆

Endlessly wet and dreary weather

SCOTLAND HAS PROVIDED MANY valued benefits to the world, ranging from porridge to penicillin, Scotch whisky to the steam engine, tarmac to the telephone. Given that the wettest place in the whole of Europe is Scotland's western Highlands, it is not surprising that they have also given us the most memorable and evocative word to describe persistently dull, wet, cold, dreary and unforgiving weather.

Dreich (*DREECH*, with the final *ch* pronounced as in *loch*) is an ancient word. Scandinavian in origin, it originally meant tedious or protracted, like a job that drags on and on, a book that doesn't know when to end, or a long and boring sermon. The novelist and poet George Macdonald referred in the late nineteenth century to 'The kirk, whan the minister's dreich and dry.'[13] He was a minister himself, so he presumably knew what he was talking about. This sense of delay, or an unwillingness to get to a conclusion, led to another phrase, *dreich in drawin'*, which could be applied to someone who seemed to be taking an unreasonable time to make a decision – a suitor, in particular, who showed no sign of wanting to get married.

That meaning of apparent endlessness is still there in the word *dreich* when it is used about the weather – the thing about a *dreich* day, apart from the cold, the sunlessness and the miserable, soaking drizzle, is that it seems as if it's never going to end. To call it particularly *Scottish* weather might be a gross libel on a country which, whatever the statistics say, has palm trees growing on the Ayrshire coast, but it remains a favourite word for Scottish poets describing the place where they live. Alexander Gray, for instance, in his poem 'December Gloaming',[14] writes movingly of the gloominess of the shortening days as the year draws to a close and the cold *dreich* winter days when night is falling at four in the afternoon. And a recent poll to establish the Scottish nation's favourite home-grown word resulted in a runaway victory for *dreich*, with nearly a quarter of the total votes cast.

What makes it especially attractive is its onomatopoeic quality – its long-drawn-out vowel sound, followed by the back-of-the-throat *ch*, as in *loch* or *Auchtermuchty*, seems to echo a *yeeuch* of disgust and resignation – two words which, in regard to the weather at least, demonstrate how much the Scots and English have in common. And yet *dreich* was lost to standard

It seems as if it's never going to end.

English centuries ago. That's odd, given that one of the distinguishing traits of the Anglo-Saxon peoples is their ability to talk so long, so passionately and so tediously about the weather. Maybe it's because the English, unlike the more realistic Scots, tend to cling even on the dullest days to an unreasonably optimistic belief that there is a tiny patch of blue sky and it'll brighten up yet.

Perhaps *dreich* is a word that Scots can safely use about Scotland, but the English had better not. And to tread even more dangerous territory as to whether *dreich* might relate to anything deeply rooted in the Scottish character is a subject for a braver book than this one. However, it's worth remembering P. G. Wodehouse's assertion that 'It is never difficult to distinguish between a Scotsman with a grievance and a ray of sunshine.'[15]

Hozh'q

(Navajo)

♦

A deep, wholehearted appreciation of the beauty of the world

WE LIKE TO SAY that beauty is in the eye of the beholder, and when we do we may think that we have said something profound. But we don't really believe the words – after all, we read books of critical theory and listen to experts telling us what is a good painting or a fine poem. So perhaps it would be truer to say that, for most people, beauty is what's *put* in the eye of the beholder. Once we start to unpick the sentence, we can begin to see how unsatisfactory it really is.

The eye, marvellous as it is, sees only the surface of things. But what if we think of beauty as a quality that we not only see with our eyes but also experience deep within our souls? Does it affect our lives? Can it change our view of the world, transform us into different people?

The Navajo of the south-western United States would answer all these questions with an unqualified 'Yes'. Their word *hozh'q* (*HOH-shkuh*) describes the way that the beauty of the external world is seen and appreciated by each individual for himself, not only in his eyes but in his heart. It is no less than a guide for living a fulfilling life. It is an ideal – but an attainable ideal. Beauty, it says, is an essentially subjective and personal concept, and in finding it and experiencing it in both heart and soul, an individual learns what is important to him or her.

The nineteenth-century artist, designer, poet and novelist William Morris offered a golden rule: 'Have nothing in your life that you do not know to be useful or believe to be beautiful.'[16] The Navajo of his day might not have accepted the distinction between what is useful and what is beautiful, but, in the unlikely event that they ever heard what Morris said, they would have understood his advice. *Hozh'q* would remove from life the search for wealth, material goods and social advancement, and replace it with a deep, wholehearted and transformational appreciation of the beauty of the world.

The beauty of the external world is appreciated not only in his eyes but in his heart.

Put like that, *hozh'q* sounds like an ideal philosophy and a sobering corrective to today's grab-and-go lifestyle, but it is hard to imagine many takers for it in the modern world. So is it possible to have a little *hozh'q* in your life? Is it something you can train yourself to develop in your character, like patience or tolerance, or is it an all-or-nothing concept, like virginity?

The Navajo might say the latter, but if we could borrow the concept along with the word, I can't see why it shouldn't become a part of our daily lives. When people retire from their day job, they often adopt a whole different range of priorities. Getting and having becomes a lot less important than seeing, hearing, doing and enjoying. But most of us don't think about beauty that often. The concept of *hozh'q* might remind us that there's more out there than just the things we own and the contents of our bank accounts.

Gökotta

(Swedish)

◆

An early-morning excursion to enjoy the start of a new day

IT HAS TO BE one of the best things in the world. It's early morning and for most people the day hasn't even started. A new sun is rising and you can feel the air getting warmer by the minute, perhaps there's dew on the grass, and all around you is the sound of birdsong. Not just the birds but the whole world is waking up.

In Sweden, they call that trip out into the early morning *gökotta* (*yer-KOHT-ta*). The word means literally 'early-morning cuckoo', and it strictly refers to such a trip taken specifically on Ascension Day, some six weeks after Easter. Traditionally, it's a time for early-morning picnics in a clearing in the forest, in the hope of hearing the cuckoo, which usually arrives back in Sweden from its winter migration sometime during May. The direction from which you hear its call and the number of times that you hear it are supposed to mean good or back luck.

But the Swedes love the countryside in all its manifest-ations, whether it's the wilderness, the crashing rivers and the mountain peaks of the north, the rolling countryside and endless beaches of the south, or the forests that cover two-thirds of the country. It's no surprise that a tradition like this, which celebrates the accessibility and friendliness of nature, should have spread to cover any early-morning excursion, at any time of the year.

In English, we might extend the meaning of the word even further, to cover any trip out which involves getting up early and going outside to enjoy the start of the day and the sounds that it brings. The cuckoo has always been special in England just as in Sweden, because of its shyness, its distinctive call and the regularity with which it arrives and departs with the spring and early summer. Two hundred years ago, William Wordsworth wrote about it:

Oh blithe newcomer! I have heard,
I hear thee and rejoice.
Oh cuckoo! shall I call thee Bird,
Or but a wandering Voice?[17]

Our love of this seasonal visitor goes back for centuries. But perhaps you don't need the cuckoo for a *gökotta*, though if you're lucky enough to hear one, it's a real bonus. Out in the countryside, there are still plenty of songbirds to reward you with the different sounds of their various calls, and there is still the unmistakable sense of a new day starting and the world coming to life.

We could go still further in redefining *gökotta*: not many countries, after all, are as rural as Sweden, and many people in the English-speaking world would find it impossible to reach a secluded forest glen early in the morning. So why not enjoy a *gökotta* in a town or city, just to celebrate a spring morning? The distinctive birdsong and sounds of nature won't be there – although some of the parks in London or other big cities might provide something close – but there are other sounds and experiences that are peculiar to early morning in an urban environment.

A new day starting and the world coming to life.

The rattle of shutters going up as shops start opening for business, the scrape and thud of boxes being moved inside off the pavement, the shuffle of half-asleep feet and the thunder of an early-morning bus aren't quite the traditional sounds of a Swedish *gökotta*, but there would still be the warmth of the sun and the sense of the world starting up afresh. Spring is the spring, sunshine is sunshine, and early morning is early morning wherever you are. What's not to like?

CULTURAL
CONNOTATIONS

Nemawashi

(Japanese)

♦

Behind-the-scenes networking to get everyone onside, particularly ahead of a business meeting

F OR CENTURIES, THE JAPANESE have created gardens – stylized, formal and traditional oases of calm – to encourage contemplation, provide refuge from a busy life, or simply as places where they could stroll and enjoy the peaceful sounds of running water and the breeze in the trees. They have, along the way, perfected the art of *bonsai*, the delicate cultivation of miniature trees that goes back for at least fifteen hundred years.

Both these skills demand patience, forethought, careful planning and, crucially, the development of specific techniques to achieve the result the designer wishes. Such a technique is *nemawashi*.

Nemawashi (*neh-MAOU-a-shi*) means, literally, 'going around the roots' and refers to the painstaking process by which a tree is prepared to be transplanted into the place that has been assigned to it in the overall design. The roots will be exposed one by one and carefully prepared for the trauma of being dug up and moved, so that the whole tree remains healthy and vigorous in its new location.

In its modern sense, *nemawashi* describes the equally

delicate and important process of getting ready for a meeting. Using the same image we could say, rather more prosaically, that it's the process of 'preparing the ground'. But the Japanese go about it in a much more determined and systematic way.

There will be one-to-one talks with people who are to be present, so that their support can be guaranteed and their ideas incorporated into the proposal. Senior members of the management team will expect to be informed and consulted in advance, and small groups from the whole decision-making team may be set up to hold preparatory discussions. The key to all these activities is their informality, before the all-important full meeting. It's all about sharing information, reaching a consensus and at all costs avoiding argument and public loss of face.

It's a search for new insights, new ways of refining and improving the proposal.

It also widens the pool of people whose opinions and contributions are sought. In the Toyota Production System, devised by the car-making giant as a consistent and efficient process to be followed in all their factories, *nemawashi* is seen as the first step in reaching any important decision. It often involves consulting all the employees about a new plan, from shop floor to boardroom, and aiming, in theory at least, at a company-wide consensus.

The expectation is that before anyone brings a proposal to a formal meeting, they will have carried out *nemawashi* to get a wide range of views about it and understand the problem from as many viewpoints as possible. But it is more than just a one-off event, a preparation for a specific meeting. It's built into the whole way of working, from top to bottom, of a Japanese company.

For example, a detailed study of the way a production line in a factory works may reveal a small change that could be made to improve efficiency, but before the team who carried out the research make their formal proposal, they will take the idea to the shop-floor workers who run the line, to the fork-lift drivers who move products from place to place, and to the supervisors who have day-to-day control of the whole process. Management will still make the ultimate decision but in the knowledge that everyone involved will have had a chance to fine-tune the idea.

It involves sharing, not owning, ideas at the very earliest stage. It's a search for new insights, new ways of refining and improving the proposal.

Would simply adopting the word lead to a more inclusive, more consultative style of management in companies in the English-speaking world? Might it help the search for improved productivity in British industry? Those would be big claims for a single word. But the best reason for incorporating *nemawashi* into English is simply because of where it comes from. It's a word that takes a centuries-old technique from the peaceful and relaxed world of oriental gardening and applies it to the hectic modern world of industry and manufacturing. Now that's a good idea.

Andrapodismos

(Ancient Greek)

◆

Brutal, systematic murder with no pretence otherwise

THE ANCIENT GREEKS GAVE us democracy, and philosophy, and drama, and mathematics, and the Olympic Games. They were, we've been told, a gentle, thoughtful and literate people who laid the foundations of Western civilization, engaging in deep intellectual and artistic conversation as they strolled around the agora in the centre of Athens.

If they needed any help with their public relations in a later, busier and noisier age, they could have called on John Keats in the nineteenth century, with his 'Ode on a Grecian Urn', the 'still unravish'd bride of quietness'.

'Beauty is truth, truth beauty,' he said, as he gazed in wonder at the handiwork of the Ancient Greek artist, 'that is all Ye know on earth, and all ye need to know.'[18] And we finish the poem in a warm, comforting glow, thinking fondly of the sensitive race of men who inspired such moving thoughts.

Well, yes. But the Ancient Greeks also gave us *andrapodismos (AND-ra-pod-IS-mos)*. It's a word they used to describe what they did sometimes when they conquered a city – killing all the men and selling the women and children into slavery. They weren't always quite as gentle and cerebral as we like to think.

If you wanted to translate the word into English, then 'ethnic cleansing' might be as good a phrase as any with which to start. But *andrapodismos* is more specific and also less coy. Whereas the term 'ethnic cleansing' hides its brutality behind words that might almost suggest a harmless clean-up operation with mops and buckets, *andrapodismos* is quite clear about what it means. It makes, to use an unfortunate phrase, no bones about its murderous intent.

The historian Thucydides describes a warning in 416BC from the Athenians to the island of Melos in the Cyclades, which had challenged their authority. 'The strong do what they can and the weak suffer what they must,' they told them – and then proceeded to prove it with an *andrapodismos*. Grown men were put to death and women and children sold as slaves, and, a little later, five hundred Athenian colonists arrived to seize the island for themselves.[19] The Melians should have known better: a few years before, Athens had done much the same to the people of Skione, and the Spartans carried out an *andrapodismos* at the city of Plataea. Philosophical and artistic they may have been, but the Greeks could be as brutal and bloody as any soldier in any war.

Luckily, we don't often need a word to describe such cold-blooded savagery. We know mass murder when we read about it and, God forbid, see it. And yet it's still one that would be worth its place in the dictionary, if only because of what it reminds us about the Ancient Greeks and the way we often think about them. This is not to say that they were worse than us – and names like Srebrenica, Rwanda, Islamic State and Cambodia should stifle any tendency towards that sort of complacency – but it does suggest something that we should have known all along. Perhaps they were no better, either.

We often like to believe things that we know aren't true – standing in a crowded bus or on the Underground with our faces pressed lovingly into a stranger's armpit, we might entertain wistful thoughts about what a happy life our forefathers must have enjoyed. In the sunny, unstressed, rural days before the industrial revolution, we dream, how they must have relished the summer sun as they worked in the fields by day, sleeping the sleep of the just by night. And then we remember what a cruel life of unrelieved poverty and hard work it must really have been.

It's easy to forget that humans are complicated creatures and always have been – that those we admire and respect are seldom angels and those we hate are less than the devil. Maybe 'an *andrapodismos* moment' would be a good phrase to describe those occasions when our fantasies bump up inconveniently and painfully against the truth.

Honne & Tatemae

(Japanese)

◆

A person's private and public faces – how we really feel, and the mask we show to the world

ENGLISH LIKES TO THINK of itself as a bluff, honest, John Bull of a language that says what it means and means what it says. Words that suggest that we may tell lies or misrepresent ourselves – 'hypocritical', for instance, 'insincere', 'double-dealing' or 'duplicitous' – all leave a sour taste in the mouth. Who wants to be thought a hypocrite?

And yet it doesn't always reflect the way that we behave. We all occasionally sacrifice the harsh truth in favour of the kinder, gentler, or just the easier thing to say.

Pollsters' surveys report that voters want one thing – high public spending, perhaps, even with the taxes to pay for it – but they regularly go into the privacy of the polling booth to vote for something completely different. Honesty and straightforwardness sound a much less attractive option to the man faced with the classic question, 'Does my bum look big in this?' 'Delicious,' we will say to a waiter, before smuggling pieces of inedible gristle into a paper napkin to slip into our pockets.

We have no word to suggest that there may be perfectly

honourable reasons for being less than completely truthful – privacy perhaps, or a sense of decency, or an unwillingness to cause hurt. Kindness is a virtue just as much as honesty.

Japanese is possibly the only language with words to describe such behaviour. *Honne* (*HON-NEH*) is the way you really feel, the thoughts and feelings that you will only express to your closest confidants. For everyone else, there is *tatemae* (*tat-eh-MY-eh*), the face that we show to the public – respectable, polite, cool and revealing nothing about our true feelings. The Japanese business contact to whom you explain your proposals may nod and smile and say 'Hai, hai,' – but whatever the Japanese phrasebook may say, the words do not really mean 'Yes, yes.' They mean simply, 'I hear you.'

'We must do lunch,' they may say, brightly, without intending any such thing.

Honne is to be kept carefully guarded. It might include your deepest dreams and wishes, your personal opinions and, crucially, your real emotions. It would take a long time and a lot of building of trust before foreigners – *gaijin* or *gaikokujin*, which literally means 'outsider people' – would be likely to share *honne*.

Learning to understand this difference between *honne* and *tatemae*, to adjust your speech to fit the person you are talking to, is one of the key lessons of social etiquette for Japanese children. The distinction runs through Japanese society, from the behaviour of politicians and government officials to relations between business contacts to daily social interactions.

It's important, too, to recognize how you are being spoken to. An invitation for a meal, for instance, might be *tatemae*, a purely formal mark of courtesy that is not meant to be taken up. English speakers do much the same thing – 'We must do lunch,' they may say, brightly, without intending any such thing – but they have no word to describe what they are doing. It's not about being deceitful but about not wanting to give offence.

Politeness and courtesy are built into Japanese society, and the distinction between *honne* and *tatemae* is also a virtue in its own right. One of the teachings of Confucius is that neither happiness nor anger should be apparent in one's face, and a traditional Japanese would consider it a shameful breach of good manners to express his true feelings or intentions directly. Such behaviour might be described as *baka shoujiki*, or honesty to the point of fool-ishness, and it would be seen as naive, impolite and childish.

So the Japanese, having understood and codified behaviour that the languages of the rest of the world seem to prefer to ignore, must presumably be relaxed and at ease with themselves? Sadly, no. Some social commentators agonize over fears that the rest of the world sees them as dishonest or insincere. So, as foreign travel grows more popular and Western influences increase, Japan might begin to move away from the twin concepts of *honne* and *tatemae*. Yet while English speakers value politeness, gentleness and consideration for other people's feelings just as much as the Japanese, perhaps what's needed is not for Japan to abandon the words but for them to be adopted into English to describe a practice for which we need feel no embarrassment.

Ubuntu

(Bantu)

◆

The quality of being a decent human being in relation to others and therefore of benefit to society as a whole

THE MUSIC OF BEETHOVEN, the poetry of Shakespeare, the paintings of Van Gogh – it seems somehow wrong to think of them as German, English or Dutch. They belong to all of us because they remind us what we are all, as human beings, capable of at the very summit of our potential. And the same is true of the southern African Bantu word *ubuntu* (*u-BUN-tu*, where the *u* sounds are rounded like a Yorkshireman asking for 'some butter').

Translated literally, it means the quality of being human – humanity, if you like. But that goes almost nowhere towards explaining the ramifications of what has grown into a cross between a world view, a moral aspiration and a political philosophy in southern Africa. And even that leaves out most of the associations that have grown around the word from the principles of the anti-apartheid movement and the achievements of Nelson Mandela.

When Mandela tried to explain the concept of *ubuntu*, he used a memory from his childhood of how a traveller reaching a village would never have to ask for food, shelter and entertainment. The villagers would come out and greet him and welcome him as one of them. That, said Mandela, was one aspect of *ubuntu*. It didn't mean, he went on, that people should not make the most of their own lives and enrich themselves – the important thing was that they should do so in order to enable the community as a whole to improve.

His colleague in the fight against apartheid, Archbishop Desmond Tutu, also spoke about *ubuntu* in a speech in 2007.[20] 'In our culture, there is no such thing as a solitary individual,' he said. 'We say, a person is a person through other persons – that we belong in the bundle of life. I want you to be all you can be, because that's the only way I can be all I can be.'

Ubuntu can also be a personal quality – an individual might be described as 'having *ubuntu*', in which case they have an instinctive awareness of the importance of inter-dependence. They will stand by their social obligations and be as conscious of their duties as they are of their rights; they will be aware of whatever personal qualities they possess, such as beauty or wisdom, but only in relation to other people. They may be ambitious, as Mandela suggested, but along with that ambition will go a sense that the community as a whole should profit from their advancement.

However, it is as a view of the world, a prescription for how people should behave, that *ubuntu* is best known. It is a philosophy, not a religion, as it's occasionally described – there is no supernatural element in it, no aspect of duty towards an all-powerful being, but simply a joyful recognition of the importance of community. It's important to stress that it is not a matter of unselfishly subjugating one's personal interests to those of wider society, as a communist might enjoin; rather, *ubuntu* is all about the development and fulfilment of a person's potential both as an individual and as part of a community.

In the years leading up to the collapse of apartheid in South Africa in 1994, there was a widespread conviction across the rest of the world that the country was heading for a bloodbath. But though there was violence – sporadic fighting between rival opposition groups, outbreaks of tribal antagonism, the shooting of twenty-nine people by troops in the so-called Ciskei homeland in 1992 and car bombs in Johannesburg – the widely expected wholesale slaughter never happened.

One aspect of *ubuntu* is that it specifically renounces vengeance. Many leaders of the anti-apartheid movement,

'In our culture, there is no such thing as a solitary individual.'

Mandela and Tutu among them, believed that freedom would benefit not only blacks but whites as well – freeing the jailer as well as the prisoner. More than twenty years later, South Africa remains a nation beset by problems, but *ubuntu* – described by President Barack Obama as 'Mandela's greatest gift'[21] – is a living tribute to the commitment to a sense of common purpose that transcends politics and race.

You don't need to be South African or, more specifically, a black South African to appreciate *ubuntu*. Like Beethoven's music, Shakespeare's poetry and Van Gogh's paintings, it is an inspiring reminder of what we might be capable of at our best.

Insha'allah

(Arabic)

♦

Literally 'God willing' . . . but also works well as a
brush-off, because nothing happens unless God
wants it to happen

THERE ARE PHRASES IN several languages that reflect
something of the meaning of the Arabic *insha'allah*
(*insha-all-AH*) – God willing in English, of course, or the
Latin *deo volente*. The Spanish and Portuguese words *ojalà*
and *oxalà*, with their echo of the Arabic, carry a dim 500-
year memory of Moorish rule in Iberia; and the Welsh *os
mynn duw* is a Celtic version of the same idea. But none of
them has the same deep, universal resonance of *insha'allah*.

The word Islam itself means submission – submission
to the will of God, that is – and through the whole religion
runs a rich vein of fatalism. Nothing, the devout Muslim
believes, will happen unless God wishes it to, and so it is
sinful to promise anything without acknowledging that
only the will of God can bring it about. The precise phrase
comes from a verse in the Qur'an, which warns: 'Never say
of anything, "Indeed, I will do that tomorrow," except
[when adding], "If Allah wills [*Insha'allah*]."'

To that extent, then, the phrase carries with it a sense of

the all-pervading influence of religion on a Muslim's life – a brief prayer inserted into the most mundane of remarks. But it can also be used by the less devout as a way of avoiding responsibility or commitment. If all is in God's hands, the speaker cannot be held responsible if things go wrong.

If you call on an Arab businessman in his office and his secretary tells you that he will see you later, '*insha'allah*', then you are in for a long and probably fruitless wait. In this sense, the word might be best translated by the Spanish *mañana*, which literally means 'tomorrow', but more often has a feeling about it of 'maybe tomorrow, maybe the next day, maybe never'. Between those two meanings of *insha'allah*, between the devout prayer and the smiling brush-off, lies a trap for the incautious non-Muslim.

There is a story of a wise and experienced Western businessman who fell into this trap when visiting a client to get across the message that a bill that had been outstanding for several months might usefully be paid. He was greeted with smiles, coffee and lengthy enquiries about the health of his family, and questions about the bill were brushed away as a mere nothing that should not be allowed to interrupt this pleasant reunion of old friends.

'It is nothing,' said the client from behind his large desk, with an expansive wave of his hand. 'Do not worry about this. The cheque will be signed tomorrow, *insha'allah*.'

The businessman, who had given up a whole morning to make this visit, and who had hoped to leave with a signed cheque safely in his pocket, was unimpressed. Since it was the man behind the desk, not Allah, who was going to sign the cheque, he suggested pointedly, the matter could be settled even more quickly. Like now.

And suddenly the atmosphere was different. Where there had earlier been warmth and conviviality, there was now icy formality. Instead of a relaxed conversation about an acknowledged debt that was to be paid, there was now a tense and unsmiling exchange about his lack of respect, his apparent frivolity about deeply held religious feelings and the hurt that he had caused.

The matter went no further and – several weeks later – he got his money. But he never forgot the lesson he had learned about the dangers of *insha'allah*.

Veline

(Italian)

◆

The job title of the glamorous young dancers employed to deliver the news – on sheets of paper – to male newsreaders

I T WOULD BE A dull old world if everywhere were just the same. What inspires a sharp intake of breath and a sucked-lemon expression in one place is likely to be greeted with whistles of approval, stamping feet and raucous laughter in another.

Take *veline* (*vel-EE-neh*), for instance. It's an old Italian word that, back in mediaeval times, used to mean the fine calfskin on which manuscripts were written – the same stuff that was called vellum in English. From there, it was a short journey to thin paper, and today sheets of tissue paper are referred to as *veline*. But the word developed another, more specialized, sense. During the last century, it came to be used specifically for the thin sheets of paper on which carbon copies were made – piles of them famously emanated from the offices of the Fascist government of Benito Mussolini, with official statements and decrees.

Then and afterwards, they featured prominently in newsrooms, where multiple copies of stories were rewritten and circulated as they developed. In English, they were called flimsies, which remains a good translation in more ways than one for the way the word *veline* has evolved in Italian.

The magic of computerization has replaced the endless flow of updates carried by copy-boys, runners or harassed television producers, but back in the 1980s, the Italian television channel Canale 5 launched a satirical, irreverent news programme called *Striscia la Notizia*. The word *notizia* means news, and *striscia* can be either a comic strip or a line of cocaine, which tells you something about the character of the programme. We're talking a mixture of *Mock the Week* and *The Daily Show with Jon Stewart* rather than the evening news. But one of its most notable features was that stories were carried to the newsreader onscreen by slim and sexy young dancers – the *veline*. The word flimsy was applicable not just to the papers they carried but also to the clothes that they wore.

And that is how the word *veline* gained its modern meaning. The people who produced Virgil, the Roman Empire, the Renaissance, Leonardo da Vinci and Michelangelo gave us a new word for half-naked young women dancing across the studio clutching the details of the latest Cabinet appointments or news of the economy. 'Bimbos', we might say in English.

But 'bimbos' has too much of an air of disapproval to work well as a translation. Bimbo isn't a word that suggests that a woman might have a university degree or political ambitions. No young woman is going to describe herself as a bimbo, but in Italy the *veline* developed a culture and a popularity of their own. Under the premiership of Silvio Berlusconi – who owned Canale 5 – several of his personal favourites among the *veline* without any discernible political experience appeared as candidates for the European Parliament or were appointed to high-profile positions in local and national government. This was the golden age of *velinismo*, or bimbo-ism.

Before we get too judgemental, perhaps we should remember that in England Page 3 no longer simply means what comes between Page 2 and Page 4. Famous or infamous, depending on your point of view, over the past forty-five years the *Sun* newspaper's bare-breasted glamour models have given the phrase 'Page 3' a meaning of its own. They also, like the

> The word flimsy was applicable not just to the papers they carried but also to the clothes that they wore.

veline, became famous for their pronouncements on the news stories of the day. The British have form when it comes to sexism in advertising and the news media.

However, Page 3 girls, popular as they have been, haven't yet started appearing on the benches of the House of Commons. The regional Police and Crime Commissioner or the head of the Drinking Water Inspectorate are unlikely to supplement their incomes by leaping around on a television screen in their underwear. *Veline* is not a word we're often going to need in English, but it might still be better than the sneering superiority of 'bimbo'.

Perhaps *veline* would just sound a little gentler – more relaxed and less critical of the people we're talking about and how they earn their living. And some of us at least would find that a distinct improvement.

Krengjai

(Thai)

◆

An acute awareness of other people's feelings; a desire to make others feel comfortable

In Thailand, a bizarre dance ritual is performed at almost every Western embassy function. The guests arrive – a visiting trade delegation from the UK, perhaps, and a number of potential contacts from the local Thai community – and drinks and canapés are served. And then the conversations start, about business or politics – serious stuff.

The Western guests approach to what feels like a comfortable distance from the Thais and begin to talk; the Thais, embarrassed to have someone standing so unreasonably far away from them, shuffle forward a few inches. The Westerners, puzzled at this advance, retreat away from them, and the Thais, smiling politely but feeling as if they are having a long-distance conversation by loudhailer from one ship to another, advance again. And so it goes on, with little groups of Westerners moving slowly backwards around the room, followed by the earnest and well-meaning Thais.

The problem is simply that neither side appreciates the

expectations of the other in relation to their personal space. What seems to someone used to Western drinks parties to be a reasonable distance to stand apart is a peculiar experience for the Thais. Wanting to be friendly and welcoming, they move forward – and so the dance begins. It's hard to understand local customs that are so deeply ingrained that they are seldom talked about. And so it is with *krengjai*.

To outsiders, the ancient Thai system of *krengjai* (*kreng-JEYE*) may seem to be little more than formalized deference – a stultifying sense of hierarchy that affects every area of life. And it's true that, traditionally, teachers, parents, company directors, senior police officers and other high-ranking government servants and officials would expect to be treated with respect, homage, reverence and even fear by their juniors. It would be rude and inappropriate to criticize them or even question their decisions – and extremely unfriendly to stand so far away from them while they had a conversation. But that is only a small part of *krengjai*.

Sometimes it's translated as consideration, but that is a feeble echo of the way the word resonates in Thailand. To a Thai, *krengjai* is an all-embracing concern to demonstrate awareness of other people's feelings, to show them politeness and respect and never to make them lose face. The word literally means 'respect-heart', and it involves not just surface courtesy or deference but a deeply felt desire to make people feel comfortable and at ease.

Foreign tourists sometimes claim that if you ask a Thai a direct question – 'Is this the bus for Phuket?' for instance –

he will be unwilling because of *krengjai* to disappoint you by saying no. The safest way to find out if it is the bus for Phuket, the story goes, is to ask where it is bound, without giving a hint of where you want to go. Similarly, tradesmen may agree to appointments that they have no intention of keeping, just to avoid the embarrassment of a refusal. These examples are a misunderstanding of a feeling that reflects Buddhist ideas that one should not seek fulfilment for oneself but concentrate on achieving happiness for others. In Thailand, thoughtlessness, selfishness or unkindness are deep and lasting disgraces.

Understanding the way other people see the world is one of those things, like playing with your children, watching the sun set, or smiling, that are simple, unalloyed good and positive things to do. Perhaps having the word *krengjai* in English could help to achieve that understanding in some small way. If it did, it would certainly make the world a happier place.

Inat

(Serbian)

◆

A stubborn expression of courage, often with nationalistic associations

B ACK IN 1999, WHEN NATO's bombs were showering down on Belgrade, the Serbian word *inat* (*EE-nat*) became a favourite of Western journalists trying to explain the frustrating refusal of the Serb inhabitants to do what was obviously in their best interests and surrender. Civilians were walking the streets with paper targets pinned to their chests in a 'Come and 'ave a go if you think you're 'ard enough' challenge to the pilots thousands of feet above them. One report described a Serb fighter boasting about how he would tackle the bombers with his pistol. Runners in the Belgrade marathon dodged potholes as they ran past the ruined buildings of the city, determined to finish the race, bombs or no bombs.

It was, journalists suggested, all down to *inat* – a word inherited from Turkish after centuries of Ottoman occupation, which means spite or stubbornness. But, as they were keen to explain, it means a lot more than that as well.

Inat has a sense of having your back to the wall, of being determined not to do what is asked of you. *Inat* suggests you are ready to cut off your nose to spite your face, and your ears and lips as well, if that will make your point. It's an absolute refusal to countenance surrender. If chivalry, gallantry and all the panoply of military virtues traditionally belong to the wealthy and privileged, then perhaps *inat* is a stolidly peasant expression of stoic courage.

It would be a mistake to see it as an emotion that is only expressed in wartime. A schoolboy being bullied who turns to face his attackers, ready to be beaten up but not to do whatever it is that they want from him, is driven by *inat*. So is the worker who is pushed too far by an overbearing boss and finally tells him in no uncertain terms exactly where he can stick his job. So is the driver in a narrow lane who refuses to reverse out of the way of another car, because he reckons that he was there first. Later, as they mop their bloody nose, clear their desk or inspect the scratches on their car, they may well feel a twinge of regret, but there will always be a defiant little bit of them feeling that they did what had to be done.

> A dangerous hard drug for a government to feed its people.

In a war, though, *inat* really comes into its own, and it is seized upon by governments who have little else to offer their people. As the bombs fell on Belgrade in 1999, the *inat* of the people fed into the story of a defiantly Christian race under attack down the centuries from a succession of powerful and brutal outside forces, and so it conveniently stilled the voices that might otherwise have been heard from civilians demanding how the hell the government had got them into this mess. A lot of people thought at the time that the strongly nationalist government of President Slobodan Milosevic was quietly encouraging this upsurge of *inat* as a specifically Serbian unifying force of national pride.

Inat, in fact, can be a dangerous hard drug for a government to feed its people, building up a feeling of persecution, a resentment of outsiders and a sense that it is us against the world – catnip for potentially violent nationalists.

In 1999, there was nothing specifically Serb about either the emotion or the government's exploitation of it. For people anywhere in the world sitting terrified under a modern bombardment of high explosives, fire and shards of red-hot metal, the only realistic alternatives are probably blind panic and a dogged stubbornness that takes no account of life or death but is just determined not to give in. Much the same feelings were encouraged, for much the same reasons of fostering implacable and defiant nationalism and improving morale, in the London of 1940, when the battered inhabitants looked out on the devastation of the Blitz and snarled, at least according to a government propaganda film, 'We can take it.' In fact, the most famous expression of *inat* is in English, not Serbian: 'We shall fight on the beaches, we shall fight on the landing grounds, we shall fight in the fields and in the streets. We shall fight in the hills. We shall never surrender . . .'

The British government of 1940, like their Serbian

counterparts nearly sixty years later, knew how effective *inat* could be at improving morale among a battered and frightened population. The thing about hard drugs, whether fed from a syringe or from a politician speaking over the radio, is that they may be dangerous when abused but they are very effective indeed when the patient is in real and mortal danger.

Muruwah

(Arabic)

◆

Selfless generosity associated with manliness

WILFRED THESIGER, THE GREAT Arabian traveller of the twentieth century, was constantly astounded by the generosity of the tribesmen who were his hosts and guides on his journeys across the Arabian Desert. Theirs, he said many years after his travels were over, was the only society in which he had found true nobility.

But one incident above all gave him an insight into the traditional values by which the Arabs set such store. He and his companions were joined at their camp one night by a skinny old man in a tattered and grubby loincloth, who sat down to eat with them. Thesiger was astonished at the warmth of the welcome extended to the old man by the tribesmen.

He was, one of his guides explained, a man who was known far and wide for his generosity. Thesiger was not surprised by much about the Arabs, but he looked at the old man quizzically – the bones visible beneath the skin on his half-starved body, the broken sheath of his old dagger, the clear signs of grinding poverty – and he wondered what on earth the man could have to be generous with.

His companion shook his head. This, he explained, had once been the richest man of his tribe, but now his goats and his camels were gone. He had nothing. What had happened, asked Thesiger, still not understanding. Disease? Raiders? No, came the reply. He had given them all away, killing his last animals to feed strangers he had met in the desert. He was ruined by his own generosity.

'By God, he is generous,' the tribesman said with envy in his voice, and Thesiger finally understood.

The quality the old man possessed was *muruwah*. It is usually translated as 'manliness' – a term with all sorts of cultural connotations. For us, manliness might imply a collection of adjectives such as virile, strong, vigorous and hardy, but for the Arabs, scraping a meagre living in harsh and ever-threatening conditions, it carried those meanings and far more besides. It celebrated the virtues of the desert – courage, patience and endurance – and an acceptance that the individual would sacrifice his own interests for those of the community as a whole. There was an unquestioning loyalty to the sheikh and the elders of the tribe: to ensure survival, *muruwah* (*moo-ROO-ah*, where the first is as in book, the second as in cool) had to be essentially a communal rather than an individual virtue.

It could be brutal – within the tribe, it led to an implacable adherence to traditional eye-for-an-eye justice. If a member of the tribe killed a man's camel, then his own camel would be forfeit; in a society without locks, the few possessions the tribesmen owned had to be protected with an iron law. And it went further: if someone killed a man's son, then his own child would be put to death as well. Towards those outside the tribe, it would mean at the very best a guarded hostility: *muruwah* meant that the tribesman would be ready to avenge any insult or aggression from another tribe with immediate armed retaliation.

But it embraced, too, a wholehearted generosity – a quality that was needed where there was never enough of anything. Providing food and shelter for the stranger was a matter of honour for the tribe and the individual alike; there was an instinctive egalitarianism that meant that the old, the young and the sick would be protected for as long as they could be without endangering the survival of the tribe as a whole.

> An acceptance that the individual would sacrifice his own interests for those of the community as a whole.

For centuries, *muruwah* was the only way to maintain some sort of social order among the chaos of warring tribes. It was a chivalric code of honour that dated back well before the time of Mohammed and the dawn of Islam, and, as Thesiger found, it lasted well into the twentieth century.

Taken away from its birthplace, perhaps the complexity of qualities that *muruwah* entailed is less easy to understand – in the Arabian desert, shortage of food meant that you starved, while for most people in today's developed world it probably means that you've forgotten to go to the supermarket.

But not for everyone. Even in today's wealthy countries within Europe and in the US there are people without enough to eat, and across the wider world the problem of hunger and famine is always with us. If we had a word for manliness that included an idea of generosity and social responsibility it might just encourage us to act accordingly.

Philotimo

(Greek)

◆

The love of honour

WE ALL LIKE TO feel special – even unique. Jews are the Chosen People; Britain (or maybe England, or possibly the United Kingdom – the details are a little vague) is the Mother of the Free, whom God made mighty and whose bounds shall be set 'wider still and wider'; the United States of America is the Land of Opportunity. And *philotimo* is the unique birthright of the Greeks.

Philotimo (*fill-oh-TEEM-oh*) means, literally, 'the love of honour' – to which rather grandiose phrase William Shakespeare's Falstaff might unheroically reply, 'What is honour? A word. What is in that word honour? What is that honour? Air.'[22] Those lines might not go down too well in Greece, as *philotimo* is a quality that many Greeks might say lies at the heart of who they are.

Thales of Miletus, one of the Seven Sages of Ancient Greece, observed in the early sixth century BC that *philotimo* came naturally to the Greeks. It was, he said, like breathing. 'A Greek is not a Greek without it. He might as well not be alive.' It is a quality that the Greeks frequently claim even today – a way of identifying their modern way of life with the glories of Classical Greece. And it is a mistake to be too cynical about it – *philotimo* is the quality that is often ascribed to the Greek partisans of the Second World War who risked the firing squad to help Allied servicemen and to join the resistance against the Nazi occupation. For them, it was much more than a fine word. The reply to Falstaff might be that honour, in their case, involved personal pride, honesty, courage and a passionate sense of freedom coupled with a deeply felt patriotism.

Philotimo is a quality that many Greeks might say lies at the heart of who they are.

But these qualities, central to *philotimo*, don't tell the whole story. Over the centuries, it has come to represent a number of virtues that are seen as typically Greek – not just generosity but also appreciation of the generosity of others; not just love for your family but delight in their love for you; not just freedom but a sense of the limits placed on your freedom by your own instinct for what is right. In particular, it involves an understanding of the right way to behave in your relationships with others, whether within your own family or in wider society. *Philotimo* brings together the private individual and the public man.

The trouble is that these virtues, which describe the qualities that make an ideal man or woman, are universal – there can be few nations in the world that have not, at some time or other, claimed them as their own. In his first letter to the Thessalonians, the people of Thessalonica, St

Paul urged them to live their lives with *philotimo* – a message that was passed on through the Bible to all the people of Christendom. The Greeks may not have a monopoly on the virtues, but they do have the only word to describe them. We can't all be Greeks, but we can all achieve *philotimo*.

NUTS AND BOLTS

Fartlek

(Swedish)

◆

Alternating fast and slow running

IT'S NOT MUCH OF a secret. Inside each one of us, hidden deep in the recesses of our inner psyche, is an eight-year-old child trying to get out. He or she isn't altogether happy with all that adult stuff, like jobs, ambition and politics, which seems to fill so much of our lives. What this inner child likes is fun, laughter, chocolate biscuits and an occasional guilty snigger at something that seems rather harmlessly grubby.

Every now and then, that inner eight-year-old needs to be let out to play. And this is where the Swedish word *fartlek* (FART-laik) comes in. It literally means 'speed-play' and describes a type of athletics training devised in the 1930s in which periods of fast and slow running are intermingled. It doesn't take much to imagine organized lines of unsmiling, blond-bearded Swedish athletes conscientiously counting their paces as they jog and then sprint and then jog again up and down snow-covered Swedish mountains with unpronounceable names, but it's those first four letters that give *fartlek* its shame-faced appeal in English.

It's a word that can't be spoken without giving that

inner eight-year-old, who is generally kept so carefully hidden, the opportunity for a vulgar snigger. But there's more to *fartlek* than that. Words remind us of our history – the *k* and the *gh* in *knight* are distant echoes of the Anglo-Saxon pronunciation, and the Hindi roots of *bungalow* are a memory of the British Raj in India. Similarly, *fartlek* invokes the past in a very direct way, taking us a great deal further back than the memory of our eight-year-old selves. If the *fart* part gives us a cheap laugh, the *lek* part carries a hidden reminder to English speakers of their Norse heritage.

Lek survives – just – in Yorkshire dialect, where it means play, just as it does in Swedish. It has survived from the Old Norse of the Vikings for more than a thousand years, lurking on the borders of English ever since the raiders swarmed ashore, raping and pillaging and spreading carnage and chaos across the land. If we were ever to allow the little twist of Viking DNA that's buried in our genome to clap on its horned helmet, grab its battleaxe and rampage through our quiet streets, we would end up at the very least in the magistrates' court. We're not going to seize a bullock from a field and carry it off to roast over an open fire, washed down with flagons of fiery alcohol drunk from a human skull. We're not going to leap out of the car and hack down the traffic lights that seem to have been holding us up for ever. We're not going to fly with whirling axe and savage war cry at the annoying little man who tells us to keep off the grass. But it's good to be reminded by that one little word that those things are there in our DNA, just waiting to be let out. We could if we wanted to.

A case might be made for adopting *fartlek* into English because it could be useful to have a word that describes a mixture of running and walking – hurrying for a bus, for instance, when you're not fit enough to sprint all the way to the bus stop, and, anyway, you're carrying heavy shopping. But the real reason is much simpler. It reminds us, in two very different ways, of who we used to be.

Desenrascanço

(Portuguese)

◆

To solve a practical problem using only the materials to hand

I T'S PROBABLY ONE OF the most important skills a person can learn and yet there is no satisfactory word for it in English.

The Portuguese speak of *desenrascanço* (*d'AYS-en-ras-CAN-sauo*), which literally means 'disentanglement' but is used to describe the ability to put together a last-minute, emergency solution to a problem by using the materials that happen to be available. It may not last, you may well not be using the various component parts of the solution in accordance with the manufacturers' instructions, and don't even mention health and safety, but whatever idea it is that you've cobbled together will at least get you home. Probably.

You are driving home late at night, and you hear an ominous metallic crash from the back of the car, immediately followed by a scraping sound, possibly with a glimpse of sparks flying up off the road flashing into your rear-view mirror. The exhaust pipe that you have been meaning to fix for weeks has finally come adrift, and you are stranded.

If you are the sort of English speaker who lives life

according to a series of instructions, such as 'Be Prepared' or 'Fail to prepare, prepare to fail', rather than the concept of *desenrascanço*, then this doesn't apply to you. You will have had the exhaust fixed in the first place, or at the very least you will have had the foresight to pack a complete tool kit, together with a pair of overalls, safely in the back of the car. If, on the other hand, you are like most people, you will call out a breakdown service and sit for an hour and a half in the cold while they try to find you.

But if you are Portuguese, you will take off your leather belt, wrap it around the exhaust pipe and fiddle it through the exhaust bracket or some other convenient part of the underside of your car. As you drive home, you can mentally pat yourself on the back and ponder on the meaning of *desenrascanço*.

It's not limited to cars. *Desenrascanço* can be applied to problems with your computer, with household equipment, gardening tools or anything else that can go wrong. You can use it to recover lost keys from a drain or replace vital items of equipment. Some people might even try it, optimistically, when attempting to save faltering relationships.

It involves inventiveness, imagination and flexibility, as well as the sort of confidence that believes there is no practical problem in the word that cannot be solved with a wire coat hanger, a piece of string, a little bit of sticky tape and a lot of ingenuity. An unwillingness to spend money is also an advantage – one thing that skilled practitioners of *desenrascanço* have in common is an expression of horrified disbelief when they see the price of manufacturers' spare parts or skilled repairmen.

There is, however, a significant disadvantage to the whole idea. If you are less than proficient in the necessary skill, or a little clumsy with your hands, your repair will go wrong and some smart Alec will tell you that whatever it is you've been fixing is *farpotshket (see p. 147)*. You will then end up having to pay someone to do the job properly, and it will cost you much more time and money than if you'd got help in the first place. Sound familiar?

Lagom

(Swedish)

•

Not too much or too little, but just the right amount

I N RECENT BRITISH POLITICS, one phrase has been overused to such an extent that people have started to scream in anger at the television screen or the radio, perhaps even the printed page, whenever they hear it.

It doesn't matter which political party is speaking. Every revamped policy, every change in taxation rates, every new benefit proposal, every fresh idea, has been aimed at the 'hard-working family'. It seems to have been generally agreed among political speechwriters that everyone who is anyone wants to work hard to get ahead and achieve a better life for their family. Americans, in the same way, never tire of telling you that anyone, however poor their birth, can achieve staggering, limitless, mind-blowing wealth. Yachts, mansions, private jets, swimming pools and an annual income equivalent to the GDP of a medium-sized nation – they are all up for grabs, with a bit of hard work. That, they insist, is not a myth but the American Dream.

It's very likely that most Swedes wouldn't understand. Like everyone else, they see the virtue of hard work and appreciate the benefits of ambition, but the Swedes also see that scrabbling as fast as you can for money and advancement has a downside. Not only are you likely to trample on other people as you elbow your way up, you also tend to miss out on a lot of things like time with your family, relationships, reading a book or just sitting smelling the flowers. The word that most Swedes would choose to sum up their attitude to life would be *lagom* (*la-GOHM*).

Lagom is used to express satisfaction, and if you ask a group of Swedes for a word that encapsulates the essence of living in Sweden, that's the one they would probably choose. It means just right, not too much or too little – but without the rather grudging air of 'satisfactory' or 'sufficient' in English. How are you? *Lagom*. Is your coffee hot enough? *Lagom*. How's the weather? *Lagom*. Someone's height may be *lagom*, so may the number of people at a party.

It's a positive word, and many Swedes would extend its use from the expression of satisfaction with the amount of food on their plate to describing the nature of Sweden's politics. It's a social democratic, middle-of-the-road country where taxes are high and people might find it hard to get rich, but where everyone is looked after and life is . . . well, *lagom*. It means equality and fairness: there is enough for everyone.

Work–life balance is important to the Swedes. Whereas in the City of London or on Wall Street, burned-out executives are reputed to leave jackets over their chairs when they stagger home after a sixteen-hour day so that people will think they've just slipped out for a moment and are still working at their desks, in Stockholm that would simply cause bemusement. If you have to work such long hours, it means that you've planned your work badly, they would think. Your career, too, should be *lagom*.

Clearly they're doing something right, because Sweden always figures at or around the top of the league tables that are produced periodically, setting out the countries where people are happiest and most content. And in London, too, perhaps there seems to be a shift of emphasis away from chasing the last commission and towards aiming to be home in time to put the children to bed. Younger people are less ready to sell themselves body and soul to the company in the way that their parents' generation did.

So maybe *lagom* is a word that the English language is waiting for. Would it be a good thing to have it in the dictionary? Well, not too good, not too bad. Just *lagom*.

Epibreren

(Dutch)

◆

**Unspecified activities which give the appearance
of being busy and important in the workplace**

TECHNOLOGY, AS WE ALL know, makes simple things more
complicated.

In big bureaucracies like the Civil Service, the EU or
the BBC, all you once needed to get to the top were brackets
after your job title and a clipboard – the brackets to prove
you were important, and the clipboard to prove you were
busy.

The brackets were the most important part of your official role. If you were a simple News Editor at the BBC, you
were expected to perform some comparatively menial task
such as editing news. If your title was Editor (News), then
the brackets told the world that you were a person of
substance, who would be involved in strategic blue-sky
thinking, analysis and inter-departmental relations, rather
than actually *doing* anything. You would no more dream of
editing news than you would of washing up the coffee
cups. You have to be important before you can be
successful.

But even though you avoided doing anything, you had

to look busy. You had to give the appearance of being pro-active and decisive as you strode confidently down the corridor from the morning medium-term forward planning symposium to the Performance Analysis Unit. Nothing was better for that than being armed with a clipboard. You could stop and make notes on it occasionally, but the clipboard itself would do the trick.

But now clipboards belong in a museum. They've been replaced by tablet computers and smart phones – and since *everyone* has those, and no one can tell whether you are devising strategically vital spreadsheets on them or checking your Facebook page, they're no use at all for making you look important.

What you need these days is *epibreren*.

Epibreren (*ep-i-BREER-un*) is a Dutch word originally coined by the newspaper columnist Simon

But even though you avoided doing anything, you had to look busy.

Carmiggelt, and it means – well, it means nothing at all. That is the beauty of it. Carmiggelt claimed in one of his columns that the word had been revealed to him in 1953 by a civil servant from whom he had requested some papers. The papers, said the civil servant, still needed *epibreren*. Intrigued, Carmiggelt asked what *epibreren* meant, and the civil servant eventually confessed that it had no meaning. It was a word he had made up to fend off enquiries.

The story is almost certainly just that – a story.

Carmiggelt was a talented columnist with a column to fill. But the word *epibreren* survived and has come to refer to unspecified activities that sound as though they might be important but don't actually amount to anything. In short, it's a catch-all excuse for inaction, laziness or inefficiency, which also manages to make the speaker sound rather grand. The theory is that people never like to admit that they don't understand what someone has said, so if the excuse is given with sufficient confidence and in crisp efficient tones which suggest that the speaker has very important things that he or she has to be getting on with, it's likely to be accepted. But it's more than just an excuse – not only does it fob off enquiries, it also makes you look like a person of stature, someone at the top of the food chain. It's the verbal equivalent of the once-ubiquitous clipboard.

We're much less subtle in English. Our excuses, such as 'The cheque is in the post' or 'My computer has gone down', are so crude that they generally aren't even meant to be believed. 'The dog ate my homework.' The problem with them is they indicate an acceptance that something is wrong, even though they pass the blame on to someone or something else. The beauty of *epibreren* is that it reflects the fault back on to the complainer – 'Can't you understand how important this is?' it seems to say. 'How could you be so inconsiderate as to waste my valuable time with these petty questions?' It has just the sort of empty, airy superiority that a senior executive needs.

Perhaps we could adapt the word to describe all vacuous attempts to avoid responsibility? Who knows, in a few years' time, most big bureaucracies could even have a Department of *Epibreren*. And the head of department will be referred to as Senior Executive (*Epibreren*) – don't forget those brackets.

Poronkusema

(Finnish)

◆

**An old unit of measurement equivalent
to the distance travelled by a reindeer
before needing to urinate**

I F YOU HAVE ANY idea what a rod, pole or perch is, the
chances are that you are English and over fifty years of
age. If you're a little younger – especially if you are interested in horse racing – you might do better with a furlong,
while a cricketer might be able to advise you about a chain.
And most people could probably manage to describe an
acre, even though they might not be too sure how big it
was.

They're all old units of measurement that date back to
the centuries before anyone thought of measuring how far
it is from the equator to the North Pole, dividing the answer
by ten million and calling the result a metre. They belong
to an older, slower and less accurate age when measure-
ments related to the way that people lived their lives, rather
than to abstract calculations performed in laboratories by
scientists in white coats. They all go back to the mediaeval
ploughman driving his oxen over the field.

The team was expected to plod on ploughing its furrow

until it had to rest – a distance that was reckoned to be about 220 yards (just over 200 metres) and which therefore became known as a furrowlong, or furlong. The stick with which the ploughman controlled the oxen had to be five and a half yards long (just over five metres) to reach the front pair – one rod long. Put four of those rods end to end and you reach the width of the area that the team aimed to plough in a day. *That* distance became known as a chain in the seventeenth century, when surveyors started to use chains as the most accurate way to measure it, and survives as the length of a cricket pitch. Multiply the length of a furrow (220 yards) by a chain (22 yards), and you have an acre (4,840 square yards), the area a team was expected to plough in day. Do the maths and marvel.

It all sounds complicated and slightly arbitrary today, but it wouldn't have done in the times when men went out to plough the fields every day. Then, the units would have chimed with the way they lived their lives. And the same was true for the herdsmen who drove reindeer across the wastes of northern Finland. Their unit of measurement was even more down to earth.

A *poronkusema* (*por-on-koo-SAY-mah*) was the distance that a reindeer was believed to be capable of travelling without stopping for a pee. If you're interested – and if you were herding the animals, you would be – it's about 7.5 kilometres. It was in official use as a measurement of distance until metrication in the late nineteenth century.

It's unlikely, in the twenty-first century, we're ever going to need to know the distance that we can drive a reindeer along a motorway until we need a reindeer service station. The *poronkusema* is obsolete in more ways than one. But perhaps it's worth a new lease of life as a way of describing something like a typewriter or those dusty antique farm-workers' tools that you sometimes see hanging on the walls of country pubs – something that is old and outdated, it's true, but which reminds us nostalgically of past times.

Farpotshket

(Yiddish)

•

Irreparable damage to something caused by a botched attempt to mend it

I<small>T MAY SEEM HARD</small> for anyone under fifty to believe, but there was a day when an ordinary person could open the bonnet of a car and have at least a sporting chance of understanding what they found there. They could fiddle with the engine, tweak it a bit, even fix it when it went wrong. Not today, of course – everything is governed by a computer that can only be reset by a piece of equipment that costs a fortune and needs a graduate in electronic engineering to make it work.

You could drive a car on which the clutch linkage was made out of a twisted wire coat hanger, or use a pair of tights as a fan belt (while hoping your mother didn't miss them). You might even have broken an egg into the radiator in an attempt to fix a water leak. But those are far-off golden days, when the summers were warmer and the chocolate bars bigger and tastier. And the memories of how we used to raise the car's bonnet and work magic with the engine are a little rose-tinted, too.

The description that comes to mind for these attempted

running repairs is not do-it-yourself wizard or ad hoc genius but *farpotshket*.

Try as you might to pretend differently, not only did these fixes not work (except for the coat hanger and the clutch – that modification could be carried out by an expert and the car would work for years), they ended in disaster. *Farpotshket* (*fahr-POTS-SKEHT*) is a Yiddish word which describes something that is irreparably damaged as a result of ham-fisted attempts to mend it.

It's the second part of that definition that makes the word such a delight. It's not just that it doesn't work – that would be bad enough but easily described with the American military acronym SNAFU (Situation Normal: All – umm – Fouled Up). The point about something being *farpotshket* is that you messed it up yourself, or you trusted someone else to do it and they messed it up for you. There is something hair-tearingly infuriating about it – the word carries with it just an echo of the superior sniggering of the experts who could have done it all so much better, if only you'd paid them. But more than anything, it comes with the resigned shrugged shoulder of a person who knows that he should have known better. It was never going to work.

It has an associated verb that is almost as expressive – *potshky* (*POTs-ski*) is to fiddle with something in a well-meaning and purposeful way but with a complete lack of competence. You can *potshky* with anything – cars and other machines, of course, but also with intangible things like diary arrangements, things you have written, or even relationships. What they have in common is that once you have *potshky*-ed with them, they will collapse in disarray. And it will all be your own fault.

Cars, computers, electronic devices – the relevance of *farpotshket* to daily life today is obvious. 'It looks simple enough – that little wire seems to have come adrift. If I just connect it *there* . . .' BANG! And then you call the helpline and a concerned voice on the other side of the world says, 'Well, as long as you didn't . . . Oh, that *is* what you did. Well, it's *farpotshket* then.' Or at least they would if we could say that in English.

Tassa

(Swedish)

◆

A silent, cautious, prowling walk – like that of a cat

CATS, FOR ALL THE pictures on the Internet showing them looking cute with ribbons around their necks and peering winningly over the edge of a cardboard box, are carefully designed killing machines. The merciless green eyes give nothing away; the claws that can rip off a mouse's head with a single flick are delicately sheathed out of sight in those silky soft paws; and the creature proceeds stealthily, one foot placed precisely in front of another, as it makes its silky, sinuous way towards its prey.

It's a way of moving that we sometimes try to emulate, perhaps in order to avoid waking someone up or disturbing them while they are concentrating or listening to music. Perhaps, if we are of a particularly infantile turn of mind, we simply want to creep up behind them and say 'Boo'.

We might tiptoe, but we might also put our heel to the ground first and then carefully roll down the outside of our foot until our weight is on the ball of the foot, walking silently like a moccasin-clad Native American making his way through the forest. And the reason that this way of walking has to be so carefully described is that we simply don't have a word for it.

Or at least we do, but we use it differently – 'pussy-footing' would be an ideal word to describe walking like a cat, but we've invested that with its own incongruous meaning. You can't imagine a cat 'pussyfooting' around its prey. Delicate and infinitely cautious they may be, but when they are hunting they move straight towards their dinner.

The Swedes have a much better word. *Tass* (*TASS*) is an animal's paw and *tassa* (*tas-SAH*) is the verb meaning to walk silently and delicately, like an animal. It is quite distinct from either 'tiptoe' or 'pad' – the two words in English that might be used most commonly to translate it. Tiptoeing, by contrast, sounds crude and clunky. The noun 'pad' – meaning the sole of an animal's foot, which we turn into a verb in order to say 'padding around' – has none of the sense of silence, caution and deliberation that *tassa* carries with it. It's partly the sound of the word – that double-s in the middle has the effect of a finger to the lips and a quiet 'sshhh!'

But it's not only about silence – it's about control. When a cat puts its foot to the ground, it instinctively checks the firmness beneath before it transfers its weight. It could, if it needed to, lift the foot again without losing its balance. Only the muscles needed for movement are under any tension – the rest of the animal's body is relaxed and at ease. There is a subtle muscular control that, for a human, would be almost reminiscent of the flowing Chinese martial art of tai chi. *Tassa* is to move like that – silently, with liquid grace and total control.

It's never going to be a common word – it has a specialized and very precise meaning. *Tassa* is not the way we move around every day. It is never going to be used to describe how we walk to the pub or carry the rubbish out to the bins. But as we creep upstairs late at night, or try not to wake the baby, or avoid disturbing the teenager at her homework, *tassa* is the word that should be on our mind.

Tsundoku

(Japanese)

◆

A pile of books waiting to be read

BOOK LOVERS ALL HAVE the same guilty secret. And they all dread the same question when people see their collection of books.

'So have you read them all?'

It's a perfectly civil question and quite flattering, since it suggests that all the information, knowledge and wisdom distilled in the pages on your shelves might just be replicated in your brain, but it makes most booklovers quail. Because the honest answer, for most of us, is 'No'.

How can you explain about the book that you bought when you were passionately interested in a particular subject, only to find when you got it home that it was as dull as last month's newspaper? Or the ones that you snapped up on a whim in the bookshop because their covers looked so appealing? Or the ones – a growing number as you get older – that you might possibly have read years ago, if only you could now remember the tiniest hint of what they contain. Or the ones you were given as presents, which you never much liked from the moment you opened the parcel. When the excuses run out, the answer is the same.

There are books on our shelves that we haven't read.

We will read them one day, we tell ourselves with the best of intentions, and so we keep them in convenient piles around the room or next to our bed. When we have time, we say, or we promise ourselves a few days off, or we keep a pile ready for our summer holiday and another for when we wake in the night. But somehow, inexplicably, the piles just keep growing.

This practice, as the Japanese will tell you, is *tsundoku* (*TSOON-do-coo*). It literally means 'reading pile', but it's used to describe the act of piling up books and leaving them unread around your house. To those not infected with the book-collecting bug, the tottering and apparently random piles may seem to be nothing but an unsightly mess, but the dedicated practitioner of *tsundoku* will know where each book is as clearly as if they were catalogued by computer.

You could expand the word's meaning to cover any of the pleasant actions that we mean to take one day – the visits to old friends, the things we're going to buy, the holidays in exotic countries. They're not something to beat ourselves up about, because piling up treats to fill the future is one of the best things about being alive. There is no shame in those piles of books that you will read – perhaps – when you have the chance.

If we had no *tsundoku* in our lives, it would indeed be a bleak and cheerless world.

Only Human
After All

Shemomechama

(Georgian)

◆

The embarrassing sudden realization that, somehow, you've eaten it all . . .

IN ENGLISH, WE HAVE words and we put them together to form a sentence. There can be very short sentences – 'I ran', say, or 'I slept'. But the shortness of these sentences is a result of their simplicity, not the cleverness of the words themselves. In Georgia, they do things differently. They can tell a whole story, all in a single word.

Shemomechama (*shem-o-meh-DJAHM-uh*) means 'I didn't mean to, but I suddenly found I had eaten all of it.' It may not be an entirely convincing plea from a small boy standing in front of you with an empty plate and a guilty expression, but it's an impressively complex idea to get across in a single word.

They can manage it largely because Georgian – one of a small group of languages in the Caucasus, with its own delicate and elegant script – has a number of varied and expressive prefixes, which can add subtle shades of meaning to the most simple verbs. So in this case, the *mechama* part of the word means 'I had eaten', but the *shemo* prefix combines an expression of desire, a reluctance to fulfil that desire and then a slightly shame-faced, shoulder-shrugging admission that temptation was too great.

Not even the Georgians can squeeze into that word a full explanation for *why* you've been so weak – maybe the food was particularly tasty, maybe you were unbearably hungry, or maybe you just kept nibbling away with your mind on other things and suddenly discovered to your horror that you'd eaten the lot. But that probably doesn't matter – trying to come up with a reason isn't going to make it any better as an excuse. Whoever you're telling is still going to be pretty cross, although probably not as cross as in two other examples of the same prefix at work.

The first, *shemomelakha* (*shem-o-meh-LAKH-uh*), is the sort of thing you might say to the magistrate. It means, worryingly, 'I only meant to rough him up a little, but I somehow found I had beaten him half to death.' And the second, which could also get you into serious trouble, is *shemometqvna* (*shem-o-meh-TKV'N-uh*), which is not used in polite society and means something like 'I was only thinking of a quick kiss and cuddle to begin with, but I somehow ended up . . . Well, the flesh is weak.'

Lewis Carroll, author of *Alice in Wonderland*, invented the term 'portmanteau word' to describe the idea of two meanings packed into a single word, like the two halves of a large suitcase. To carry on the metaphor, *shemo* is not even a word in its own right but deserves to be thought of as a whole matched set of luggage. It is a triumph of compression.

English speakers are unlikely to get their tongues round the complexities of *shemomechama* – and, incidentally, if you think that Georgian is hard to pronounce, you should see the script. (The Romans, who knew a thing or two about empires and foreign cultures, wrote the language off as incomprehensible.) But with due apologies for butchering their language, we might borrow the prefix and use it on its own, to mean 'I didn't meant to, but somehow it just happened . . .' – whatever 'it' might be.

'Did you realize that you were doing 40 mph in a 30 mph zone, madam?' And the reply is a guilty shake of the head and a muttered, '*Shemo.*'

'You said you were going to be home by seven, and it's nearly three in the morning!' How did that happen? '*Shemo.*'

Tartle

(Scots)

◆

Social faux pas of forgetting the name of the person you're introducing

No DOUBT SOMEONE, SOMEWHERE, thought years ago that they were doing the world a favour when they invented the name badge that people could wear at conferences or parties. Not only will it simplify introductions, they must have thought, it will also save the embarrassment of forgetting somebody's name.

The problem is that the people most likely to forget names are those who are middle-aged or more, and they are also the most likely to be short-sighted. The embarrassment caused by having to lean forwards and peer at a woman's chest, in particular, is far worse than an honest admission that you've forgotten her name. Better by far, the Scots might say, to *tartle* (*TAR-tll*).

Tartle originally meant to hesitate nervously, whether in meeting someone, failing to reach a business deal, or simply backing away from anything unusual, as a horse might. From that, it has developed to refer specifically to that horrifying moment when you are halfway through an introduction and forget the name of the person you are introducing. Perhaps you may remember only their first name, perhaps only their second, perhaps only a nickname, but whichever it is you are caught with a stupid smile on your face and nothing coming out of your mouth except a stream of unedifying ers and umms. You are *tartling*.

The word can be either a verb – 'I was just introducing her when I *tartled*' – or a noun – 'Please forgive my *tartle*.' Either way, it's a light-hearted and jovial way of describing an excruciating social moment.

If we are going to incorporate *tartle* into the English language, there's no reason why we should restrict the definition to the specific meaning that the Scots have given it. As we get older, many of us succumb to what we like to call 'senior moments' – we start to talk about a certain film star, singer or politician and find halfway through the sentence that we've forgotten their name. We say, incautiously, that there are three reasons for something and then start to list them – knowing, deep down in our soul, that after the second one our mind will go blank. We go into a room and then stand there bemused for a few seconds while we try to remember what we came in for.

All of these moments are different forms of *tartles*. If we could name them with a word a little more dignified than the twee 'senior moment', perhaps we would find them easier to face. If you're under thirty and can't see why on earth we would need a word like *tartle*, just wait a few years.

Amae

(Japanese)

•

Behaving in an endearingly helpless way that encourages other people to want to take care of you

So you're in your thirties – successful and making a name for yourself in your career. People at work want to know your opinion. When you say something, they listen. You are a pretty big cheese, although you would never say so yourself.

But when you travel home to see your parents, you expect the special dinner you always enjoyed as a child – and you'll let your mother see how disappointed you are if it's not on the table. You want to sleep in your own room, where the books that saw you through adolescence are still on the shelves. If you think you can get away with it, perhaps you'll take your washing home – and of course you *can* get away with it because your mother will not only wash it but also iron it, fold it and put it carefully back in your overnight bag for you.

You are suffering from a serious dose of *amae*.

Amae (*ahm-EYE*) is a Japanese word popularized by the psychoanalyst Takeo Doi in his book *The Anatomy of*

Dependence, which was published in Japan in the 1970s. It describes a type of behaviour which he claimed was particularly prevalent among the Japanese but which many Westerners will recognize in their friends. Some may also see it in themselves and feel a little embarrassed about it, but it's a word that's normally applied to other people. It refers to a tendency to curry favour or induce affection by behaving in a way that encourages other people to take care of you, and its commonest form is to continue to act like a child in dealings with your parents. Such as demanding your special meal or taking your washing home.

The parent–child relationship is for many people a model for the way they behave throughout their lives, but it's not the only place where *amae* shows itself. There are all sorts of ways in which people carry out *amae* in their working lives and in their wider personal relations. Usually it appears in a relationship between someone junior and someone senior in the workplace, or between someone younger and someone older in a social setting.

But that's not always the case. Often, it shows itself in a claimed weakness or incapacity – the woman who 'can't' change a wheel on her car and waits helplessly for some man to step forward and do it for her; the man who holds up his crumpled shirt with what he hopes is an appealing smile and simpers to the woman in his life that he 'doesn't know how' to use an iron. It's not just that they want the job done but also that they want to be loved for their helplessness. They are the walking, talking human manifestation of the famous heart-rending, head-on-one-side, big-eyed gaze of an Andrex puppy – and often they make you want to give them a good, hard kick.

But that's a very negative view, and there is a positive side to *amae*, too, especially as practised in Japan. Doi's theory was that Japanese society never completely abandons the dependent phase of childhood, so that *amae* is reflected in the strictly hierarchical structure of many companies. It may take longer to establish a close business relationship, but once it's achieved it's likely to be marked by trust on both sides and a sense of personal responsibility. And it's not just a one-way relationship.

The junior Japanese executive may profit from the advice and experience of his senior, while the older exec enjoys the respect and deference he receives and feels he deserves; the young woman in her car has her wheel changed for her, and the man who does it gets an agreeable if rather patronizing feeling of superiority.

The young woman visiting her parents, meanwhile, gets a tasty meal and a bag of freshly laundered washing. But if she steps too far out of line and demands too much, she's not too old to end up on the naughty step.

Iktsuarpok

(Inuit)

◆

The anxious and irresistible need to check whether who, or what, you're waiting for has arrived yet

IT CAN MANIFEST ITSELF in different ways.

Perhaps it's waiting for a girlfriend to arrive – just aching to see her, anticipating the arrival of the person who might turn out to be the love of your life and turn your world upside down. You start glancing at the clock about an hour before the time you've arranged. Then you check that everything is ready – that the table is laid or the glasses are out ready to pour your first drink. And then – still ages before she is due – you peep out of the window to see if she might have arrived early. And finally you actually go outside and peer up the road to see if she is on her way.

Or perhaps, more prosaically, it's standing in a bus shelter, craning your neck for the umpteenth time to see if the bus has turned the corner yet.

It's not only about anxiety – you can feel the same mounting tension even if you know for certain that the person is going to come or if you haven't got an urgent appointment that you're going to miss if the bus is late.

There's a positive feeling of excited anticipation – you want the excitement of seeing whatever it is you're waiting for as soon as you possibly can. Even so, you'll only be absolutely certain they haven't let you down once you see the person in the flesh or the bus in the road, so the little niggle of unease is there.

Whether it's a bus or the love of your life, it doesn't make sense – when they get here you'll know, and they won't arrive any more quickly because you keep leaping out of your chair or peering anxiously down the road. But you just can't help yourself.

The Inuit of northern Canada have a word for it – *iktsuarpok (ITT-suar-POHK)* – which catches precisely that excitement and the physical activity that goes with it. It's usually translated as 'the feeling of anticipation when you're expecting a visitor', but, crucially, it also contains the sense that you try to ease the tension by getting up and going out to see if they are coming.

> You want the excitement of seeing whatever it is you're waiting for as soon as you possibly can.

It could also cover those secret glances at the telephone when you're expecting a call, or the surreptitious checking of your email or Twitter feed to see if anyone has tried to contact you.

It's surreptitious because you know, deep down inside, that it's a sign of weakness, but it's an appealing sort of weakness. It's the opposite of composed self-possession

– an involuntary admission of a lack of confidence. While we're encouraged to strive to be the sort of person who breezes through life brimming with self-belief and with no thought for the possibility of failure or rejection, few of us really buy into it. So to see someone acknowledge, even with a silent downward glance at a mobile phone, that they're anxious for something to happen and worried that it might not is to realize that we're not alone in the world.

Fremdschämen

(German)

•

The empathy felt when someone else
makes a complete fool of himself

❖

Pena Ajena

(Spanish)

❖

Myötähäpeä

(Finnish)

ASK SOMEONE FOR AN example of a foreign word that can't be translated into English and they're most likely to come up with the German *Schadenfreude* (*SHAH-den-froy-duh*), which means the guilty thrill of pleasure felt when someone else comes a cropper. Think Laurel and Hardy and a custard pie or, for a more scholarly approach, you could refer to the *Summa Theologica* of the thirteenth-century philosopher and theologian St Thomas Aquinas on the eagerly anticipated delights of heaven: 'That the saints may enjoy their beatitude more thoroughly, and give more abundant thanks for it to God, a perfect sight of the punishment of the damned is granted them.'

So, among the other joys of Paradise, one might experience an eternity of heavenly *Schadenfreude* while gazing down on the suffering, tortured souls below. There's something horribly smug about the idea, but it's a word that has been picked up from the German and is quite commonly used in English, so it's clear we recognize the feeling.

A 2013 academic study in the United States concluded that taking pleasure in this way from other people's misfortunes or failures is a 'normal' human response, but that doesn't necessarily make it one we should be proud of.[23] Importantly, it's not the only response possible when we see someone making a fool of themselves.

Imagine that you are at a wedding reception and the best man rises to make his speech. You realize first from the way that he is holding on to the table for support, and then from the slight slurring of his words, that he has been a bit too free with the beers, the wine and the champagne. And then he starts to speak. It is a car crash in slow motion. The jokes would have been too vulgar even for the stag night, and here the bride's parents and her elderly relatives are starting to shift uneasily in their chairs. The bride is looking distinctly unhappy, and the groom has his head in his hands. But the best man is oblivious and ploughs drunk-enly on . . .

Well, you might feel a sneaking sense of malicious delight in his predicament – *Schadenfreude*. But you might also, in a more sympathetic spirit, shudder with embarrassment on his behalf. If the words we use reflect the emotions that we feel, it's rather worrying that we have one to describe that first unworthy feeling but nothing for the more generous response.

And yet *Schadenfreude* does have a more charitable opposite in German. *Fremdschämen (FREMT-shah-mun)* literally means 'foreign-shame', and it describes the feeling of being embarrassed on someone else's behalf – that 'No, don't do it!' feeling that you have as your drunken friend staggers to his feet. In fact, it needn't be someone that you know, and they may not even be aware of how they are letting themselves down, but you can still feel your toes start to curl in vicarious embarrassment.

The fact that we use the one German word and not the other suggests that English speakers are a peculiarly unsym-pathetic lot. Other European languages have their own words for the feeling: in Spanish it's *pena ajena (PEH-nah ackh-EYN-ah*, where the *ckh* is pronounced at the back of the throat, like the Scottish *loch*); *vergonha alheia (ver-GOHN-ya'al-EY-ya)* in Portuguese; *myötähäpeä (my-ER-ta-HAP-ey-a)* in Finnish. They all mean more or less the same thing. *Plaatsvervangende schaamte (PLAHTS-ver-VONG-EN-duh-SHAHM-tuh)* in Dutch probably has the most helpful literal translation – 'place-exchanging shame'. While in English, all we can do is shudder with embarrassment and wish for the ground to swallow us up.

To be fair, *Fremdschämen* only appeared in the German language within the last ten years, so the Germans aren't that far ahead of us, but it still means that the Spanish, the Portuguese, the Finns and the Dutch are apparently instinctively more generous and sympathetic than English speakers. Here, then, is a word to help us express our better selves.

T'aarof

(Farsi)

◆

The gentle verbal ping-pong between two people who both insist on paying and won't back down

PICTURE THE SCENE. Two friends are in a cafe, ordering at the counter and looking forward to a catch-up over some caffeine.

'That'll be £4.40, please,' says the extortionist barista.

One of the friends dives into her purse to find some cash, which she attempts to hand over. The trouble is that the other friend is unwittingly schooled in *t'aarof*, and *she* holds out some cash, too. The result is that these two women, both of them with impeccable manners, squabble like schoolgirls, pushing each other's hands aside over who is going to pay for both of them.

These 'No, let *me*' arguments over dinner bills, or rounds of drinks, or cinema tickets can be painful, and there is an alternative. You want to pay? Fine, you pay, and next time it will be my turn. It will all even up in the end, for God's sake. But that's the view of someone with no concept of *t'aarof*.

T'aarof (*TAA-ruf*) is the Farsi word for a system of etiquette that is central to social life in Iran. It involves an assumption of deference, with each party to a discussion insisting that the other is more worthy of consideration. So the most casual visitor to an Iranian home will be offered tea, or perhaps a piece of fruit, or a sweetmeat with yogurt or honey. By the rules of *t'aarof*, he will decline, and the host will repeat the offer more urgently. This can go on through several exchanges, just like the two women fighting over coffee, until one or the other weakens. (If you're supposed to be trying to turn down the sweetmeats, it's as well to make sure that you're the one who weakens. They're delicious.)

To outsiders – particularly Americans, who generally pride themselves on saying what they mean and meaning what they say – this can be confusing, but behind the courteous fencing is a genuine confusion that has to be eradicated. The host wants, above all, to be welcoming, and so offers the refreshment however inconvenient it may be. The guest, in turn, might like the drink or the food but, more than that, doesn't want to inconvenience his host. And so the exchange starts, with each side looking for clues about what the other is really thinking.

The principle extends throughout various situations. If a guest compliments his host on any of his possessions – a piece of glassware or a picture – he may well be offered it as a gift, and the same dizzying circle of refusal and increasingly pressing offer will begin. A shopkeeper may insist that the item to be bought is really worthless, whereupon a sort of reverse haggling starts, with the purchaser insisting on its value and the shopkeeper talking it down; a group of businessmen may refuse to answer a question until it is clear which one is the most senior and he has given his opinion.

Visitors to Iran are sometimes warned that the expectation is that they should refuse any offer three times, but in reality *t'aarof* is less prescriptive and more subtle than this. Deep down, it's about each party to the discussion wanting to show respect to the other. It's a phenomenon that's familiar enough in the English-speaking world and one which we ought to learn to deal with rather than squirm over. Perhaps if we had a word for it – like *t'aarof* – we might manage the embarrassment of it a little better.

Kummerspeck

(German)

•

The weight gained through overeating when grief-stricken

OCCASIONALLY, POLITICIANS HAVE TO make sacrifices for their country – perhaps even put themselves through near-torture in the interests of diplomacy. In the 1980s, it was Margaret Thatcher's turn.

The Prime Minister was visiting the then German chancellor, Helmut Kohl, at his home near Ludwigshafen on the Rhine. National leaders always like to show off the culinary delicacies of their own country, and so Kohl invited her to lunch at a local tavern – not an environment in which the Iron Lady was at her most comfortable. Her idea of a good lunch was a nice piece of delicately grilled Dover sole, and she visibly blanched as her plate was piled high with *Saumagen* – stuffed pig's stomach – with mounds of sauerkraut and potatoes to go with it. She did her best but was still picking rather primly at it as Chancellor Kohl, who was known to be a monumental trencherman, returned for his second helping. And then his third. Mrs Thatcher survived the experience with her dignity and her good humour intact – just.

The point is that, fairly or unfairly, the Germans have a reputation for being expansive about their food and drink. The British are known for their love of beer, but a nation that consumes its lager from one-litre *steins* is never likely to come second in a drinking contest. And German cookery, as Mr Kohl demonstrated, is better known for the generosity of its portions than for the delicacy of its preparation.

The Germans – at least according to reputation – have never needed an excuse to grow large and imposing. Again, Chancellor Kohl might be quoted as an example. So why does a nation like that need a word like *Kummerspeck*?

Kummerspeck (*KOOM-ar-shpek*, with the *oo* as in *book*) is the Germans' ideal excuse for putting on unwanted weight. It means literally 'grief-bacon', and it refers to the extra weight gained as a result of overeating through grief. The 'bacon' part of the word (*speck*) doesn't refer to the crispy slices of heaven that go with eggs for breakfast but to the unmovable deposits of fat that build up relentlessly under your skin. But it is the 'grief' part – *kummer* – that is the masterpiece of the word as an excuse.

Kummer means grief, sadness or general sorrow. You have only to say it and you have disarmed criticism at once – what sort of person is going to make someone who has just told them that they are grief-stricken, sorrowful and world-weary feel even worse by telling them they're getting fat?

Kummerspeck acknowledges the fact that among the

most popular items of self-medication for sadness and distress are tubs of ice cream, chocolate brownies and chips, and draws attention to their fairly obvious side effects. But why does a nation like Germany, whose recipe books and restaurants suggest that they need no excuses for eating and drinking with more enthusiasm than wisdom, need an excuse anyway?

Well, so much for national stereotypes. The statistics tell a different story. They show that if anyone needs an excuse for piling on weight it's the British. English speakers in Europe – the UK and Ireland – occupy two of the top three places in the Organisation for Economic Co-operation and Development's European league table of obesity, with only Hungary above. The Germans, for all their pigs' trotters and apple strudels and immense *steins* of lager, are a svelte and highly respectable seventeenth.

Given it's the Brits who are guilty of shovelling in the fish and chips, double-size burgers and cream cakes, we *do* need an excuse for such poor eating habits, and *kummerspeck* could be the one. We should be thankful to the Germans for providing us with the word and take it to our hearts – where those fatty deposits are busy constricting our arteries – at once.

Jayus

(Indonesian)

◆

A joke so unfunny you have to laugh

WHEN YOUR CHILDREN ARE small, you want to make them laugh and be happy, and so you tell them jokes – simple jokes, the sort they'll understand, with puns and pratfalls and probably a few rude noises as well. They will want to please you in return, in the way that children do, and so, even though they haven't had the chance yet to learn what sort of things really *are* funny, they laugh.

And so you believe that you have told them a funny joke and go on to repeat the performance, again and again. That loud click you may or may not hear at around this point is the sound of the trap snapping shut: you are now telling Dad-jokes, and the habit will enslave you. Since parents never notice their children growing up, you will probably continue to do it, if they let you, well into their teens and possibly beyond. Finally, you will be telling Grandad-jokes, from which sad fate there is definitely no escape.

The Indonesians clearly understand this predicament, since they have a word to describe both the joke and the person who tells it – *jayus* (jie-OOS). It's a joke that simply isn't funny and neither is the person who tells it – a joke, in fact, that fails so completely that the hearer has to laugh because it is so bad.

It doesn't apply only to men or fathers. Teachers are another group particularly prone to *jayus*. It's a word that belongs originally to the informal language of Indonesia, *bahasa gaul*, which is generally used in day-to-day conversation and in popular newspapers and magazines, and so it's a way to deflate authority or pomposity.

It's more than just a bad or a lame joke. It may be the quality of the telling that makes a *jayus* rather than the story itself, but the laughter that it causes comes in relief that the performance is over, in surprise that anyone could tell such a bad joke, or in mockery of the poor sap who has tried so hard and so ineffectually to be funny.

It's certainly not polite, sympathetic laughter, to make the joke-teller feel better, because that would be a deliberate and purposeful decision, and the response to a *jayus* is as instinctive and irresistible as a genuine belly laugh. In fact, just like the self-deluding, joke-telling dad, the *jayus* may take the laughter at face value and continue to believe that he is a natural-born comedian.

And that, of course, is a joke in itself – just not the one he thought he was telling. The joker has become the joke, which, for all the pleasure it may give his listeners, is not a place anyone would like to be. But there are worse things to be than a *jayus*. A world that contains Dad-jokes also contains Dad-dancing. And no language on earth, thank God, has a word for that.

Guddle & Bourach

(Scots)

◆

A bit of a mess that can be sorted out & a hideous mess that is almost irreparable

BACK IN 2007, THE Scottish National Party came to power in Edinburgh after an election that had been beset by problems and controversy. In fact, commented the BBC's Scottish political editor, Brian Taylor, it had been a 'voting *guddle*' (*GUDD-ull*). But it was worse than that, he went on: 'The authorities are saying: (1) we couldn't get all the ballot papers out; (2) they were so complex, people couldn't fill them in; (3) when they finally filled them in, we couldn't count the blasted things! There's a splendid Gaelic word, *bourach*. It means an utter, hideous mess. This is *bourach*, Mach Five.'[24]

In fact, *bourach* (*BOO-rackh,* where the *ckh* is pronounced at the back of the throat, as in *loch*) has several meanings, all of them coming from the original sense of a pile or a heap. The Lanarkshire poet John Black, in his collection *Melodies and Memories*, wrote in 1909 of tea parties with 'Bourachs big o' cake and bun, to grace the feasts an' spice the fun.' It also came to mean a cluster or a small group of people, birds or animals, and at the same time a small hut, particularly one used by children to play in – presumably because such a rough hut might well look like a pile of stones.

But it's in the sense of a mess or a state of confusion that it's mostly used today, and the comparison with *guddle* helps to define both words. *Guddle* was originally a verb, which meant to grope around uncertainly under water and, more particularly, to try to catch a fish with your bare hands. From that sense of blind uncertainty, it gained the meaning that it has today. It has an attractive sound, but we have any number of words already that mean much the same thing – think of muddle, mess or jumble.

So a *bourach* is like a *guddle*, only more so.

Either one is a splendidly evocative word for a whole variety of confusions, from the organizational shambles of the Scottish election to the normal state of a teenager's bedroom, to the chaos that follows the start of roadworks on a busy street. The difference is that a *guddle* is a bit of a tangle that can be sorted with some patience and application, whereas a *bourach* is the sort of rats' nest of chaos that makes you want to throw your hands in the air and give up.

So, while a *guddle* is often something that has simply happened – nobody's fault, just an example of how things can go wrong – a *bourach* is often the result of someone's good intentions going awry. You can make a *bourach* of a place or of a job, but either way it's going to be the sort of experience that you won't forget in a hurry. Suppose, for instance, that you are baking a cake. The kitchen can often get in a bit of a *guddle*, particularly if you don't put things away and wash up as you go. You'll have a lot of tidying up and clearing to do once the cake's in the oven, but with a bit of work everything will be fine by the time it's cooked.

But now add in a four-year-old child who's desperate to help. Not only will they keep getting extra plates and cake tins out of the cupboard in case you need them, they'll also want to sift the flour for you and end up getting it all over the floor, the curtains and probably themselves. They may decide, while your back is turned, that what the cake really needs is a sprinkling of chocolate chips, but in reaching to take them down from the shelf, they'll spill most of them and eat the rest. Half a pound of sugar will vanish down the back of a cupboard, and along the way a whole bottle of milk will be spilt, two eggs will be dropped on the floor and three of your favourite dishes will end up in pieces. Between you, you will have made a complete *bourach* of the kitchen.

And then, when you forget to take the cake out of the oven, you'll have made a *bourach* of that as well.

Schnapsidee

(German)

◆

An off-the-wall idea that comes from a drinking session

GOOD IDEAS DON'T JUST come from nowhere. We all need something to spark the imagination, to get our thoughts running, and sometimes that something is a couple of drinks. Alcohol can set off all sorts of ideas, but most of them aren't good at all. Making decisions after a late-night session is seldom a sensible plan. Most of the inspiration that comes out of the neck of a bottle would have been better left deeply buried in your subconscious.

The Germans have a word for the sort of idea that results – a *schnapsidee* (*SHNAPS-i-day*) is, literally, a 'booze-idea', and it's used to describe a suggestion that is seen as completely impractical. *Schnaps* is the German for spirits or strong liquor, but the word is used even when there's no implication that the person putting forward the idea has been drinking. A young child could have a *schnapsidee*, or a teetotal church minister.

The point about a *schnapsidee* that English finds it impossible to get across in phrases such as 'hare-brained plan' or even 'midsummer madness' – which are a couple of translations that are sometimes suggested – is that it's not just a bad idea, it's an idea so ridiculous that you cannot have been thinking straight when you came up with it. It's thoughtlessly, self-indulgently stupid.

But that makes it sound like a very solemn, judgemental term, which it's not. *Schnapsidee* is generally used about less consequential ideas rather than serious issues. You might say that swimming in a river on Christmas Day is a *schnapsidee*, but a German wouldn't have used the word – even if he'd dared to – to tell Hitler what he thought of his idea of marching to Moscow.

However, it has just the degree of surprised incredulity that we sometimes want to express about grandiose political programmes: 'I just can't believe anyone could ever have thought that was a good idea!' It could apply on all sides of political divides. Calling a strike? *Schnapsidee.* Sending the police or the army to break a strike? *Schnapsidee.* Leave the European Union (or join the European Union)? *Schnapsidee.*

At the risk of getting into the dangerous area of national stereotypes, are the Germans maybe given to working things out in detail, planning, dotting every i and crossing every t? If so, perhaps that's why they've won the football World Cup four times, but it might also explain why they have such a downer on off-the-wall ideas that come out of a bottle of booze.

If we're going to steal someone else's word and make it our own, we should take the chance to be really radical.

While most ideas that come with the tang of alcohol on them would be better quietly forgotten, there are some that fly – some that come from a place deep inside us, where we have no inhibitions, where we have ideas that fizz and change the world. If a drink or two can unlock the door to that place, then we shouldn't be so keen to write off the *schnapsidee*.

Imagine a Spanish merchant in the mid-fifteenth century sharing a glass of wine on the waterfront at Palos de la Frontera with a sea captain in his forties – not a young man in those days. 'OK, Columbus, so you're planning a trip to the Indies . . . but you want to sail *which* way?' And off he wanders, shaking his head at the madness of the fool he's just been talking to, the *schnapsidee* of it all – never guessing that a new world lies somewhere over the horizon and that the 'fool' will soon be walking on its beaches.

Why shouldn't we use *schnapsidee* to mean an idea that *seems* to be wild and crazy, and leave open the possibility that it just might be a flash of the purest brilliance?

Here's to the *schnapsidee*!

Notes

1 Françoise Sagan, *La Chamade,* tr. Robert Westhoff (London: Penguin Books, 1968).

2 This unsourced story, which Dumas is said to have enjoyed, appears in several collections of anecdotes from the nineteenth century onwards.

3 A. E. Housman, *A Shropshire Lad* (1896) in *A Shropshire Lad and Other Poems,* ed. Nick Laird (London: Penguin Classics, 2010).

4 E. V. Lucas, *The Life of Charles Lamb* (London: G. P. Putnam & Sons, 1905).

5 Boris Zhitkov, *Što ja vídel* or *What I Saw,* ed. Richard L. Leed and Lora Paperno (Indiana University: Slavica Publishers, 1988).

6 *Tsurezuregusa* or *Essays in Idleness*, tr. Donald Keene (New York: Columbia University Press, 1998).

7 A. E. Housman, *A Shropshire Lad* (1896) in *A Shropshire Lad and Other Poems,* ed. Nick Laird (London: Penguin Classics, 2010).

8 Preface to *Lyrical Ballads*, 1800, in *Lyrical Ballads*, ed. Michael Mason (London: Routledge, Longman Annotated English Poets, 2007).

9 Federico García Lorca, 'Play and Theory of the Duende', published in *Lorca – In Search of Duende*, tr. Christopher Maurer (Paris: New Directions, 1998).

10 Nick Cave, *The Secret Life of the Love Song*, published in *The Complete Lyrics 1978–2007* (London: Penguin, 2007).

11 Milan Kundera, *The Book of Laughter and Forgetting* (New York: Knopf, 1980).

12 Miriam-Rose Ungunmerr-Baumann, *Dadirri: A Reflection* (http://nextwave.org.au/wp-content/uploads/Dadirri-Inner-Deep-Listening-M-R-Ungunmerr-Bauman-Refl.pdf).

13 George Macdonald, 'What the Auld Fowk are Thinkin" in *The Poetical Works of George Macdonald* (Gloucester: Dodo Press, 2007).

14 Alexander Gray, 'December Gloaming' in *Gossip – A Book of New Poems* (Edinburgh: Porpoise Press, 1928).

15 P. G. Wodehouse, *Blandings Castle* (London: Herbert Jenkins, 1935).

16 William Morris, *Hopes and Fears for Art* (London: Ellis and White, 1882).

17 William Wordsworth, 'To the Cuckoo', in *Lyrical Ballads*, ed. Michael Mason (London: Routledge, Longman Annotated English Poets, 2007).

18 John Keats, 'Ode on a Grecian Urn', in *John Keats: The Complete Poems,* ed. John Barnard (London: Penguin Classics, 1977).

19 Thucydides, *History of the Peloponnesian War,* tr. Richard Crawley (http://www.gutenberg.org/files/7142/7142-h/7142-h.htm).

20 Archbishop Desmond Tutu, 'Semester at Sea' lecture, 2007, (https://www.youtube.com/watch?v=gWZHx9DJR-M).

21 Speech at Memorial Service for Nelson Mandela (Johannesburg, 2013).

22 William Shakespeare, *Henry IV Part 1*, Act V, Scene i.

23 Professor Susan Fiske and Mina Cikara, 'Their pain, our pleasure: stereotype content and schadenfreude', *Annals of the New York Academy of Sciences*, vol. 1299, September 2013.

24 Brian Taylor, report on Holyrood election 2007 (http://www.bbc.co.uk/blogs/election07/scotland/2007/05/ah_bourach.html).

Acknowledgements

I've gone to many native speakers of different languages for help with writing this book, and also to scholars who have spent years gaining a deep understanding of a language that fascinates them. What they've all had in common is their enthusiasm – people want to share things that they find special about a language that they love.

There are too many to list them all, but I owe particular thanks to Bariya Ataya, Tamsin Craig, Elsa Davies, Eva Dingwall, Irakli Gabriadze, Orit Gadiesh, Quinten Gueurs, Ricky Lacey, Professor Vali Lalioti, Nino Madghachian, Professor Mark Riley, Wendy Robbins, Pat Roberts and Georgi Vardeli.

My agent, James Wills, and my editor, Andrea Henry, have given me the benefit of their valuable professional help; and I've enjoyed working on this book even more because from the start I've shared it, like everything else, with my wife Penny.

And finally, Dr Tim Littlewood and the NHS team in the Department of Haematology at Oxford's John Radcliffe Hospital. There really isn't a word in any language to express what you feel when people save your life.

About the Author

Andrew Taylor is a linguist of questionable skill, who speaks enough French to make the French sneer at him, enough Arabic to make Arabs laugh at him, and enough Spanish to order a cup of coffee and have a hope of getting, if not necessarily what he asked for, at least a hot drink of some kind. He can ask for milk in Russian, and if he asks for directions in the street, he will understand the answer if it means 'Straight on.' He is better at English, in which he has written ten books, including biographies and books on language, history and poetry, and he has a lot of friends who speak a wide variety of languages and who have helped him with this book.

For more information on Andrew Taylor and his books, visit his website www.andrewtaylor.uk.net